GOD'S SON, GOD'S GLORY

Emmanuel Oganla

GOD'S SON, GOD'S GLORY

Dedication

This book is dedicated to God, my family, friends and the entire body of Christ. I pray you are challenged and positively impacted as you read.

Table of Contents

Acknowledgements

First, I must give honour to God. Everything in this book would not be in it if I didn't first learn from Him. I would literally have had nothing to write.

I give thanks to my mother and father, Teleola Oganla and Michael Oganla for all their support which contributed to the writing of my book. I also want to thank my siblings (Tobi, Dare, and Gold Oganla) and my cousins (Queen and Pamilerin Olabanji) and friends who have contributed to this book: James Okoli and Michael (Entitled Music); the time you devoted to reading this book and your support are truly appreciated.

Finally, I appreciate Nia-Cerise for her contribution in writing the of the sons prayer.

Thank you for all your encouragement and support.

Introduction

Before the beginning of time, God's greatest interest was His glory. His glory compelled Him to create mankind. That is why in Isaiah 43:37, the Scripture says, **"Bring all who claim me as their God, for I have made them for my glory. It was I who created them."**

God's glory also motivated His gift of salvation towards mankind. Hence, his word affirms, **"But you are a chosen race, a royal priesthood, a holy nation, a people for His own possession, that you may proclaim the excellencies (praises of glories) of Him who called you out of darkness into His marvellous light"** (1 Peter☐ 2:5)

The issue of sonship (man's relationship with God as God's son) is the issue of the glory of God. As the Prophet Isaiah shows, this is God's intention for creating mankind and even though man sinned and fell short of the reason he was created, God offers redemption so that mankind may be with Him, and through being with Him, be empowered to glorify Him. The Bible tells a tale of a love that compels God to create mankind for His glory. God created mankind and placed him on earth to be in communion with Him. This communion is the means through which God intends to empower man to reveal His glory in the earth. God's glory is His nature, and the reason why God created man was so that His nature, which is the culture of His kingdom, will fill the domain of man (earth) as it fills God's domain (heaven). What I mean by this is simply that the kingdom of God as the Apostle Paul writes, in his second epistle to the Corinthians, is 'righteousness peace and joy.' At the same time, we understand through Paul's letter to the Galatians that two of the fruits of the spirit (which describes God's nature), are joy and peace. I will exhaust time and pages if I list the different number of times that the Bible speaks of the righteous nature of God. Therefore, God's nature, namely: righteousness, peace and joy, is the very culture of His kingdom; if man reveals God's nature, the earth will be filled with righteousness, peace and joy. As God's glory establishes the culture of heaven, it will establish earth's culture.

Where mankind failed in living in his identity as God's son and consequently failed in achieving God's purpose for creation, God became man. He clothed Himself in flesh to literally show man how it is done. Jesus Christ serves as the example of the true identity of humanity, which is sonship, and the true purpose of humanity which is God's glory. One of the purposes of His coming was to be God's Logos. Logos is the Word of God that reveals the mind and will of God. In other words, Jesus revealed God's will and intent for creation, which He achieved through the gospels. Through this book and as you take on the attitude of the Berean Christians, who heard the teachings of Paul and examined it according to scripture, you will gain revelation and understanding on your identity in God and be empowered to follow in the footsteps of Jesus.

I encourage you to not treat this as a mere book but to see it as a means of communing with the heavenly Father. When there is a specific truth that challenges you, pray! Pray against the things I address that should not be in the life of a son if they are in your life. You must not feel condemned about it as God reveals to redeem. Likewise pray into your life the truths that should be in the life of a son that you are not currently seeing in yours and you will begin to see them. I pray that as we explore the word of God you will be comforted, convicted and challenged with your true identity and purpose in God and that the lifestyle of a Son will be activated in you, In Jesus Name.

Chapter 1: The first Son

'What man lost through the first Adam, Christ has restored. Make God your all in all don't seek other gods.'

Chapter 1: The first son

In order to understand sonship, we must first understand Adam and Eve. Genesis 1 tells us that Adam and Eve were made in the image and likeness of God. This means that Adam was God's prototype on earth. The word "image" in Hebrew is Tselem, which literally translates to a shadow-like representation. Adam is the Hebrew word for man. So, when we break this down, we realise that man was made to be a visual representation of God. This is why throughout the Old Testament; God had a problem with idol worship.

God's problem with idols

Exodus 20:4

You shall not make for yourself an image in the form of anything in heaven above or on the earth beneath or in the waters below.

The reason God had a problem with the children of Israel creating images for idol worship is because they were creating a false image or representation of His identity, and He had already created the right representation of His identity, which is man.

Isaiah 45:10

Gather together and come; assemble, you fugitives from the nations.
Ignorant are those who carry about idols of wood, who pray to gods that cannot save.

This verse in Isaiah clearly illustrates how idols violate the image and representation of God because God is a Saviour. However, the idols that the people were praying to failed to display this attribute of God because they could not save.

Psalm 115:5-8

But their idols are silver and gold, made by human hands.
They have mouths, but cannot speak, eyes, but cannot see.

They have ears, but cannot hear, noses, but cannot smell.
They have hands, but cannot feel, feet, but cannot walk, nor can they utter a sound with their throats. Those who make them will be like them and so will all who trust in them.

God's problem with idols is further communicated in this verse as He is a God who spoke the world into existence.
He is also the God whose eyes go to and fro the earth and nothing is hidden from His sight. It is quite clear that God can speak, see and hear. The Scripture says, "...for the eyes of the Lord are on the righteous, and His ears are attentive to their cry" (Psalm 34:15)

The purpose of God in creating man in His image reveals the value He attaches to His glory. The word "glory" is the Greek word "Doxa" and the Hebrew word "Kabod". Both words convey God's intrinsic worth, value and essence. So, God created man in His image so that His intrinsic worth, value and essence would be communicated through His visual representation, man. This is what it means to be made for God's glory. This truth is hard to swallow because it means that God entrusted His reputation to man whom He created.

Adam was given the responsibility to effectively communicate who God is through his life, but it was impossible for him to do this apart from God. The very breath of God had to come and live in him and so God breathed into man and man became a living being. The word "breath" is the Hebrew word "Ruach", which also translates to Spirit. So, Adam became a living being because God's Spirit was dwelling in him. God's Spirit to man is what a tree is to the fruit that it bears. The tree is the source or foundation of the resource made from it, which is the fruit.

We can think of the tree as the Father and the fruit as the son. This is where the term fruit of the womb comes from. It is impossible for an apple tree to bear oranges; the fruit reveals the type and nature of the tree that bears it. In the same way, it was impossible for Adam to reveal anything other than the nature of God whilst God's breath was resident in him. Adam was the son of God. The life of God in Adam was the life that was expressed through his being.

Everything God commanded Adam to do in the garden displayed something about the nature of God.

• Naming the animals

Have you ever thought about how God entrusted Adam with the responsibility of naming the animals?

Adam never checked back with God when he thought of a name. He never said, "I'm thinking about naming this one a giraffe. What do you think, God? He just named them because he was operating in the wisdom of God.

The name of a thing is powerful because it is the means through which you identify the thing. Your name gives you an identity. Therefore in naming the animals, Adam defined the animals by telling them who they are and, in doing so, he fulfilled the purpose of his creation as a visual representation of the wisdom of God.

● Working and keeping the garden

Working and keeping the garden meant that Adam would cultivate it and, in doing so, reveal the ability of God to cultivate and nurture.

To cultivate is to prepare and use land for crops or gardening. John 15:1 gives us the relevance when Jesus said: "I am the vine and my Father is the gardener." This means that what a gardener is to a garden, the Father is to Christ. We understand that Jesus is the last Adam, therefore before the fall; God was cultivating Adam through His breath that dwelt in him. Adam himself was being nurtured by God.
 As a result, he would cultivate the garden as he was being cultivated by God.

It is evident that God saw man as a garden in the beginning because He told man to be fruitful. That is exactly what a gardener will expect from his garden. God expected man to be productive. You can't give what you don't have. The only example of cultivation that Adam had in the garden was the work God was doing in him. Again, he could only cultivate the garden because God's breath was alive in him, cultivating him.

Keeping the garden was also his work. This reveals that God is a God with an amazing work ethic, not a sluggard nor a lazy deity, like idols who do nothing. Again, images created for worship tell us nothing about God. There are countless proverbs that rebuke laziness. This is because when man is lazy, there is a violation upon the glory and the knowledge of the God who worked very hard to create the heavens and the earth.

Proverbs 20:4
The sluggard does not plow after the autumn, so he begs during the harvest and has nothing.

Proverbs 6:9-11

How long will you lie down, O sluggard? When will you arise from your sleep? A little sleep, a little slumber, a little folding of the hands to rest. Your poverty will come in like a vagabond and your need like an armed man.

Proverbs 18:9

He also who is slack in his work is brother to him who destroys.

Personally, Proverbs 18:9 has been a prime motivator for me, when it comes to exhibiting God's diligence, excellence and work ethic through my life. I believe this verse emphasises God's hatred for laziness. We understand in the gospel of John that the thief comes to steal, to kill and to destroy, and the spirit that works in the thief is the devil. Therefore, one who is lazy is a kinsman (sibling) of the same nature as the devil. This is very sobering.

● Having dominion over the earth

Adam was a son of God and God is a King, that

will make Adam a king as well (even though Adam is a man). The lion is the king of the jungle and it doesn't give birth to a gazelle. It gives birth to a cub, which will grow to become a lion and become the king of the jungle.

In having dominion over the earth, Adam was mandated to manifest the rule and reign of God over heaven. The Bible says that the heaven is the Lord's but the earth He has given to the sons of men (Psalm 115:16). This means that the dominion man had over the earth was to be an expression of the dominion God had over heaven. The word "kingdom" means the domain of the king, and the word "dominion" comes from the word domain. So, God's kingdom is His dominion over a land or a realm. Heaven is the perfect expression of God's kingdom and through His intimacy or oneness with man, His kingdom will be seen in the realm He entrusted to man as well.

God's plan was that the realm of God and man (heaven and earth) will express the marriage between Him and man. For a marriage to be a marriage biblically, you need two beings that are different. You need a man and a woman who fulfil different roles. You have the man who is the loving head, and the wife who is the submissive helper. The two come together to become one (intimate). Both are covenant partners, co-labouring to achieve the same purpose and vision. God and man are two different beings. God is the loving head and man (Adam) is the submissive helper; the two are intimate or one; they are in a covenant partnership, co-labouring to extend God's kingdom to earth as it is in heaven. This is the reason why God saw Israel, His creation, as His bride. Isaiah 54:5 simply says, "For your Maker is your husband, the LORD of hosts is His name; and your Redeemer is the Holy One of Israel; He is called the God of the whole earth."

The point here is that through Adam's submission, the earth will be submitted to heaven and the marriage between God and man would be seen through their worlds. As God kept heaven blissful and in perfect peace, Adam would also keep Eden blissful and in perfect peace; thus revealing the governance, rulership and kingship of God.

When we look at Adam in the book of Genesis,

we see God's intended identity for man as sons of God and God's reason for creating man, which is His glory. If the nature of God is not being revealed through your life, then there is no meaning to the breath you inhale and exhale. Who we are and what we are created for totally hang on this truth. God's perfect will is seeing many of His sons on earth, revealing His nature and, in doing so, extending His kingdom on earth as it is in heaven. Being rooted in your identity, intimate and submitted to God are the greatest tools to fulfilling your divine purpose on earth. Adam and Eve were doing this perfectly as long as God's breath remained in them and they remained intimate and submitted to God. However, a dramatic twist occurred; things quickly took a turn for the worse, which led to an identity crisis for all of humanity. We will explore sin and its effect in the next chapter.

Chapter 2: Redemption: learning from the firstborn son.

'You become like the one you obey: God or the devil, sin or righteousness.'

Chapter 2: The Effects of the Fall: Identity Crisis

God told Adam that the day he eats of the fruit of the tree of knowledge of good and evil was the day he would surely die. What God meant was that His breath in Adam, that made him a living being, would vacate. Thus, Adam would become a walking corpse and graveyard. We see and walk past walking graveyards every day. You and I were walking graveyards till we put our trust in Jesus and received the Holy Spirit. Adam and Eve ate from the tree and disobeyed God. So, they lost the life of God in them which gave them their identity as sons of God; consequently too, they lost their ability to glorify God by revealing His nature.

This is what Paul meant in the book of Romans when he said, "All have sinned and fallen short of the glory of God" (Romans 3:23). We must remember that Adam represents humanity. Therefore humanity sinned and fell short of God's glory. The meaning of this is that humanity fell from fulfilling its divine purpose as well as its reason for being: to glorify God and reveal His nature through human life. A purposeless man is a lifeless man. You become a walking dead when you are not living the life and fulfilling the purpose you were created for. Take an iron for example, when functioning in its proper context and fulfilling its created purpose it serves humanity; providing us with smart looking tops and trousers that make us look dashing for work, school or church. However, out of context it can be a violent weapon used to bring about death and destruction. Death and destruction can only come through a man who is lifeless because he has fallen from his divine purpose. Remember, the fruit a tree bears reveals the type of tree it is.

I gave three keys as optimum tools needed for man to fulfil his divine purpose on earth in the previous chapter. They were: identity, submission and intimacy with God. When we explore the temptation of Adam and Eve, we will see that the enemy attacked the first two keys which had significant implications for their intimacy with God.

The first thing the enemy tempted Eve to give up was her submission to God because she was tempted by the enemy to disobey God. Every kind of sin known to man has a common agenda: to attack our worship to God which encompasses our submission and obedience to His will. Think of a sin you can commit without relinquishing your submission to God. Whether it is sexual sin, hatred, slander, malice, envy, lying, stealing, gossiping and murder, they have the same thing in common. You can't be in submission to God when you are committing those acts. So when the enemy is tempting you, he is presenting to you the option of worshipping and obeying something other than God and that thing is himself. When you succumb to the temptation, for a moment you switch masters, and in doing so, you switch the context for your life and the person who defines you. Essentially, you switch your God. That was exactly what Eve did.

The second thing that the enemy attacked was Eve's identity. He said to Eve, "You will be like God." Naturally, you can only really show people what the face of your dad looks like, through your face, if you look like him. If I see an identical twin, I will know exactly what his twin looks like by looking at him. Eve could only reveal the life of God because God's life was in her. She could only manifest His life because she was like God. However, the enemy lied to her that she would be like God, if she ate the fruit of the tree of the knowledge of good and evil. The truth is that Eve was already like God. What added insult to the injury was that man traded his identity. Instead of being a son of God that looks like God and in turn could manifest Him, man became the son of the devil, took on the identity and likeness of the devil and began to manifest the enemy by producing everything that God hated through his life. It got to the point that God regretted that He made man.

Genesis 6:5-6

Then the Lord saw that the wickedness of man was great in the earth, and that every intent of the thoughts of his heart was only evil continually. And the Lord was sorry that He had made man on the earth, and He was grieved in His heart.

I believe this is because man, through his continuous acts of sin, rebellion and wickedness, reminded God of His adversary.

It was also because man, whom God made the crowning glory of His image, invested so many resources in and created to reveal His glory, had failed to fulfill a divine purpose and a glorious agenda.

Everyone has sinned and fallen short of the glory of God. As a result, we have all lived as orphans. Mankind was fathered by a liar and became a lie as a result. This is what Jesus meant when He rebuked the crowd in John 8:44 and said: "You are of your father the devil and your will is to do your father's desires. He was a murderer from the beginning, and does not stand in the truth, because there is no truth in him. When he lies, he speaks out of his own character, for he is a liar and the father of lies" (John 8:44 ESV).

The reason this occurred is because you become like the person you submit to. This makes perfect sense when you understand that worship requires conformity. Adam and Eve submitted to the voice of the devil and became like him as a result. The notion that you become like the one you submit to plays out in biblical marriages. The Bible encourages men to love their wives and women to submit to their husbands. So, submission is set in stone. Besides, the Bible says that a man will leave his father and his mother and be joined to his wife and the two shall become one. This is the picture of intimacy: they become one and alike. The wife becomes like her husband in her submission to him. In the same way, man relinquished his covenant with God, made another one with the devil and became a lie by submitting to the liar.

Adam handed the keys (authority) that God gave him over the earth to the devil. Then he began to co-labour with the devil as a submissive helper and the outcome destroyed the realm of man. The earth looked nothing like the realm of God which is heaven. Whilst order and peace reign in heaven, chaos and destruction and evil ruled the earth. According to the scriptures, "The wisdom of this world is earthly, sensual and demonic. It involves jealousy, selfish ambition, disorder and every vile practice (James 3:15-16). This is the case because man made the enemy the god of this world.

The result of disobedience to the will of God and obedience to the will of the devil is that human beings become more like the devil and nothing like God, and our world is paying the price. I have mentioned that by obeying the liar, man became a lie as a result. I would like to discuss how that truth played out in my life before my repentance.
This, I hope, will make you see how you have conformed to a lie, due to lack of submission to God.

• Bondage to sexual sin

God's will is clear when it comes to sex. Its only context is marriage.
However, growing up and being a young man in a world that is immoral, unspiritual and demonic, the norm is that there is something wrong with you, if you are not sexually active at the age of 15.
You either lie to fit in with everybody else, when they are talking about their sexual experiences, or you admit that you are a virgin who has never masturbated and be mocked and ridiculed for it.

Now, obviously we know that the role of the father is crucial, because the father is the context of the son. The first teacher of a child is his or her parent, ever before he or she goes to school. Although, I was born in a Christian home, I did not know or have a relationship with my Heavenly Father. Because of this, the only other father I knew was the devil who was subconsciously fathering me through society, in the form of peers who called me Virgin Mary in the college.

In my desire to belong and be embraced, I succumbed by losing my virginity, completely disregarding God's will and becoming a prideful, self-centered individual who used a girl's body as a means to gain approval from male friends and acquaintances in school and to appease myself.

Out of wanting to fit in, I also became a masturbator, using people made in the image and similitude of God as the objects to pleasure myself. This also had roots in being fathered and taught by the enemy and in friends who told me I was weird to be in college and not have masturbated. I gave up on the truth of who I was created to be: a son who reveals the glory of His Father. Rather, I became a lie that the enemy taught me to be.

- Materialism

Another source the enemy lied to me through was demonic doctrine. He lied to me that my worth was determined by the price of the things that I wore.
So, he also taught me to covet the guys around me who had the expensive belts and trainers.

Because I wasn't connected to my Heavenly Father and I lacked self-worth, I looked for it in people by seeking that they like the clothes that I wore. This influenced me to keep spending on items I didn't need when the will of God is radical generosity and blessing those who are in need.

I remember walking to college with brand new trainers hoping that someone would comment on them because of the nice fuzzy feeling it would produce inside. I felt heavily disappointed because no one commented.

2 Corinthians 10:12

For we dare not class ourselves or compare ourselves with those who commend themselves. But they, measuring themselves by themselves, and comparing themselves among themselves, are not wise.

As God's son, you are unique: a chosen generation a royal priesthood, a peculiar personality whom God has called to show forth His praise and glory for bringing you out of darkness into His marvellous light. Therefore, you are a pacesetter; don't compare yourself with those who are not sons. The Bible says doing so amounts to foolishness. Be wise!

It is also important for you as a son of God to know that fulfilment is not in material possession but in God. Your fulfilment is in becoming all God has created you to be and being in the centre of His will always. Your fulfilment is in your status as God's son. Those who seek fulfilment from materialism and worldly position are making a big mistake.

1 Timothy 6:17-19

As for the rich in this present age, charge them not to be haughty, nor to set their hopes on the uncertainty of riches, but on God, who richly provides us with everything to enjoy. They are to do good, to be rich in good works, to be generous and ready to share, thus storing up treasure for themselves as a good foundation for the future, so that they may take hold of that which is truly life.

One of the marks of true sons of God is that they do not find their self-worth in man, possessions or position but in God.

Psalm 139:13-14

For you formed my inward parts; you covered me in my mother's womb. I will praise you, for I am fearfully and wonderfully made; marvellous are your works, and that my soul knows very well.

Ephesians 1:3

Blessed be the God and Father of our Lord Jesus Christ, who has blessed us with every spiritual blessing in the heavenly places in Christ...

The source of your self-worth is God. He made you uniquely and exquisitely. Your physical and spiritual blessings come from Him. He is your source, the source from which all blessings flow. Sons understand this and they don't seek their self-worth outside God.

• Drunkenness, parties and the use of drugs in the university

If it was up to me, I probably would not have gone to a lot of the parties I went to. I learnt that myself, and a lot of different people can actually do without parties.

However, for fear of being an outcast, I succumbed to going to parties, smoking marijuana and getting drunk at those parties. Again, I did these things to find acceptance because I did not know the love of my Heavenly Father, who created me for His embrace. I did not know that I did not need to fit in with the world because I could perfectly rest in His arms. Living without my Heavenly Father as my context also meant I lived without restraint. I forfeited being the spirit being God created me to be for being sensual and carnal. As a result, I manifested a lie and proved that I was an orphan, being fathered by the devil.

There are many more examples I can give you about the different ways I conformed to the lie of the enemy, as a result of not knowing who God created me to be and why He put His breath in my lungs. What those two examples have in common and the reason I conformed is that I looked to find security, worth and acceptance in people.

• This looks like an addiction to social media, living for likes on Instagram pictures, Facebook status and retweets on twitter.

• It looks like a woman who is enduring the physical and verbal abuse from a man who does not know her worth, but she stays with him because her being with him makes her feel wanted and accepted.

• It looks like the young man who does not have a father figure at home and joined gangs because they made him feel as though he belonged.

• This looks like the guy who sleeps around to gain approval from peers, and the girl who constantly gives her body to guys because she wants to feel loved.

These people do not know that their worth is rooted in the fact that they were made in the image and likeness of God and the perfect love that He has for them. They do not know that they were made to be sons who display the nature of their Father through their lives.

I lived as a slave to the opinion of man. The reality is that if you are not rooted and grounded in your identity as a son of God, then you'll be an orphaned slave of man shackled to conform to who society desires you to be. This is a lie, because that's not who you were created to be. And in return, you will be receiving payment in the cheap form of momentary acceptance, worth and security. It is obviously cheap when compared to the acceptance, worth and security you receive from knowing that you are a son of God.

Romans 6:16

Do you not know that to whom you present yourselves slaves to obey, you are that one's slaves whom you obey, whether of sin leading to death, or of obedience leading to righteousness?

In the Scripture, the children of Israel did not know God as Father. So they lived as slaves continually conforming to the lifestyles of their neighbouring nations, failing to be who they were created to be and participating in the idolatry of the neighbouring nations. Rather than being the nation God set apart for Himself, they conformed to the patterns of godless and fatherless tribes.

Solomon is a prime example of a king who strayed in the idolatry of his wives. Old Testament Israel stands as a type of professed believers in the 21st century who do not know God as Father. And for that reason, conforms to the idolatry of the world in order to fit into its systems rather than being set apart from it. Whenever there is a sin issue, we must remember that it is just a symptom and the main issue is a lack of identity. You would not need to conform to the patterns of the world if you have all you need in your Heavenly Father. Also, if you're rooted in sonship, your greatest desire will be to reveal the Father.

Adam fell short of the glory of God, and we are

still seeing the effects in the world today. But thankfully, the story does not end there. The Bible says that Christ came to restore THAT which was lost.

Luke 19:10

...for the Son of Man has come to seek and to save that which was lost.

Romans 5:19
For as by one man's disobedience many were made sinners, so also by one Man's obedience many will be made righteous.

2 Corinthians 5:21
>**For He made Him who knew no sin to be sin for us, that we might become the righteousness of God in Him.**
>
>We will explore exactly what this means in the next chapter.

Chapter 3: Redemption through God's Firstborn Son (Exploring the Gospel)

'The Son of god (Jesus Christ) became the son of man, so that we the sons of men may become sons of God. That is the beauty of redemption.

Chapter 3: Redemption through God's Firstborn Son (Exploring the Gospel)

Understanding Redemption

The book of Matthew records that Christ came to save that which was lost (Matthew 18:11). This basically means that everything Man lost through sin and disobedience to God, the Firstborn Son of God (Jesus Christ) came to save, retrieve and restore it. We are used to a 'pray a prayer of repentance and you'll go from journeying to hell to journeying to heaven' kind of gospel. We are used to a gospel that tells us that Christ came to make a way for us to be forgiven from our sin but fails to tell us what redemption truly means and what it makes available for us.

What then is redemption? Well, redemption is the Greek word "apolytrosis" which means 'buying back from' or 'repurchasing what was forfeited or lost'. Therefore, Christ redeeming sinners means that Christ came to restore in man, everything Adam and Eve lost when they sinned in the garden. Adam and Eve lost their intimacy with God, their identity as sons of God and their purpose to glorify God. However, all these have been repurchased for the believer. The believers in Christ are back in the garden but never ate tree. Now the intimacy, identity and purpose of man have been restored by the death and resurrection of Jesus Christ.

The Bible says that God made the One who knew no sin to be sin that we may be the righteousness of God (2 Corinthians 5:21). Essentially, Christ became what we are so that we may become what He is. I once watched a sermon by a favourite preacher of mine called Dan Mohler. He preached a message that revolutionised my way of thinking. He quoted Isaiah 52:14, "He was marred more than any man..." In order to really understand the truth that Dan Mohler said in that sermon, which I will get to, we must consider some of the synonyms of the word marred. Some of them are: spoiled, ruined, impaired, disfigured, flawed, blemished, scarred, mutilated, defaced and deformed. This is what Dan said:

"Christ had to be beaten so bad that His appearance was deformed, disfigured and flawed. His original appearance was unrecognisable. This is because when sin took its toll on man, man looked nothing like he was created to be. His appearance was unrecognisable to God. In Christ becoming and dying as what we were, His appearance was mutilated and unrecognisable so that we may be recognisable to God again." He became what we were so we can arise as what He is, as sons. This is the beauty of redemption. We understand the true nature of redemption through Paul's second letter to the church at Corinth. In the second verse of the eleventh chapter, he said: "I feel a divine jealousy for you, since I betrothed you to one husband, to Christ, so that I might present you as a pure virgin to Christ."

The word "virgin" is pivotal in this verse because it defines someone who has never known a man or woman intimately. As a virgin is to her husband is how you are to God. You are one who is wholly devoted to Jesus, a pure bride (partner) who has never known the world. Remember the triumphal entry of Jesus to Jerusalem? "And He (Jesus) said to them, "Go into the village opposite you; and as soon as you have entered it you will find a colt tied, on which no one has sat. Lose it and bring it" (Mark 11:2 NKJV). The colt carries the presence of a person or thing. Remember, Jesus said to his disciples, "You will see a colt which no one has sat on", meaning a colt that has never carried the presence of a person.

The truth is that as human beings, we are always carrying the presence of something. We were made to be tents or temples for the presence of God. However, if we fail to carry the presence of God then we carry the presence of another (the devil and his demons). If it is not the Holy Spirit indwelling us then an unholy spirit will. We must understand that the donkey represents us, sons and daughters of God, who carry the presence of Jesus everywhere we go. Through the blood of Christ we have been redeemed. It is as though we never sinned. It is also as though we have never carried the presence of anything unholy prior to Christ. Through redemption, we have become new creations. The old us is buried in the baptism of Christ; the new us is raised to walk in the newness of life, carrying the presence of our King.

The problem with receiving the gospel that says

you should pray a prayer and go to heaven is that it positions, and encourages you to live your Christianity as though the second coming of Christ is a rescue mission rather than a return for a bride who overcame and conquered. The former sets you up to survive, whilst the latter sets you up to thrive. When you understand redemption, you will see that Christ did not only die for you because of your sins, but that He also died to remove your sins so that you may become everything God intended you to be from the beginning. It is the love of God the Father that compelled Him to send His Son, Jesus Christ, to redeem you from your sin and back to your created identity and purpose.

John 3:16, the most famous and probably the most quoted verse, tells us that God so loved the world that He gave His only son that whosoever believes in Him will not die but have everlasting life.

This tells us that there is something sending His Son tells us about the Father's love. Let's explore this.

The love of the Father

The love of the Father is expressed in that God never lost sight of who He conceived you to be in His mind, ever before you were conceived in your mother's womb and had a bodily form.

Psalm 139 put it like this, "Your eyes saw my substance, being yet unformed. And in Your book they all were written, The days fashioned for me, When as yet there were none of them" (Psalms□ 139:16□, NKJV□□□□□□□□□□□□□□□□□□□□□□□□□□□ □□□□□□).

What this means is that God the Father had a purpose for your life, ever before you had a body and walked the face of the earth. He had a purpose for your life before sin found you and took its toll on you: the purpose He had was for you to be His son - a son that is able to tell the world everything about his/her Dad.

When sin took its toll on you, God never stopped seeing what He had always intended you to be. Even now, all your sin cannot distort the way the Father sees you. He never allows what you do to undermine what He sees: His son. He sees your best potential and what you could be when He looks at you. This is one of the major drivers of God's patience which is a characteristic of His love for you.

Apostle Paul made some profound statements that all New Testament believers should note:

Ephesians 1:3-7 (NKJV)

> **Blessed be the God and Father of our Lord Jesus Christ, who has blessed us with every spiritual blessing in the heavenly places in Christ, just as He chose us in Him before the foundation of the world, that we should be holy and without blame before Him in love, having predestined us to adoption as sons by Jesus Christ to Himself, according to the good pleasure of His will, to the praise of the glory of His grace, by which He made us accepted in the Beloved. In Him we have redemption through His blood, the forgiveness of sins, according to the riches of His grace.**

We see through this passage of scripture that God predestined us, before time began to adoptions as sons.

So, His intention was for us to be sons before time began. When we forfeited our sonship and chose sin over Him, He offered us redemption through Christ Jesus because His love never fails.

This helps us to see that God's love for people is rooted in how He sees them. If I want to love people the way God loves them, then I have to see them the same way God sees me and that is as a son. Whether they know it or not, whether they are acting like it or not, I need to see them the way God saw me when I was yet a sinner and He sent His Son to die for me because of His love.

The Father of the prodigal son never stopped seeing his sons as his son. He never lost sight of who his son was, even though his son rebelled and threw away his possession. The prodigal son did not even consider himself to be a worthy son; hence he decided to go back to his father as a slave.

Even when the son lost sight of who he was, his father never did. His father restored him, putting a robe on his back, a ring on his finger and threw a big feast for him, using a slaughtered calf to grace the occasion.

The father (of the original son) never stopped having a son; he just knew that his son was lost but was pleased to find him. God sees many unbelievers the same way the father saw the prodigal son, and He is longing for the day they would be restored to Him.

Love is seeing people as the sons God sees them to be

I remember when my little cousin misbehaved and he got into trouble.
I told him to sit in the naughty corner.
After a while, he was freed from the naughty corner. However, he kept his distance from me because he was scared to come to my presence.
I called him over and he said, "I don't want to come; you're not my friend because I was naughty." I replied, "Of course, I'm your friend. I love you and you're not naughty.

You behaved in a naughty way, but that's not who you are. You are not naughty." I also told him that I am his friend, but he had to be punished because what he did was wrong.

This experience taught me about how, sometimes, we are identified by our errors and shortcomings, due to an identity crisis and failure to see ourselves the way the Father sees us. This is the reason many run away from the Father's presence when they misbehave by falling into sin. It is because, in that moment, they think that the Father does not want to be their friend. However, the way I responded to my cousin is the exact way God responds to us when we act out of character. I deliberately used the phrase 'act out of character' here because the believer must understand that their sin does not define them; it's the Father's love that defines them. Just as the Father never allows what we do to undermine what He sees, we cannot allow what we do to undermine what we see. We are the sons of the living God.

It was very important that I affirmed my little cousin's identity because a tree can only produce fruit after its own kind. Jesus said in Matthew 7 that a good tree bears good fruit and bad tree bears bad fruit. A bad tree cannot bear good fruit and a good tree cannot bear bad fruit. We must understand that the tree is the identity and the fruit is what is produced from it. If my little cousin believed that he was naughty, then his actions would always be naughty, but if he believed he was a good boy his actions would be good.

This is why the enemy works hard to tempt us away from our identity, but we fight to resist him by being rooted in it and we are rooted in our identity by our submission to God.

Remember Eve. The enemy got her to doubt her identity as a son, which made her like God, by telling her she would become like God if she ate the tree. The result was an identity crisis, the tree (Eve) became bad and its fruit (actions) was bad also. The tree she ate from and the fruit it produced, which was death, represents what we become if our identity is not in God and we disobey Him.

This is why the enemy will always try to come after your identity. He will say, "Once a sinner, always a sinner." He will get you to try to identify yourself by all the things you wish you never did or will never do because you will bear bad fruits from such attitudes. You have to see yourself the way the Father sees you and be affirmed in the new identity that He speaks over you. "You are my beloved son, and I'm pleased with you." Once you truly believe this, you will begin to live like
a son.

Value, acceptance and security are found in the love of the Father

In the previous chapter, I expounded on how a lack of identity causes individuals to conform to the lies of the enemy. I used the example of how I became someone who I was never created to be (a lie) because I wanted to feel valued and accepted by peers and society. The truth is when we see the love of the Father, expressed through the redemption brought to us by the sacrifice of Jesus Christ, our need for value; acceptance and security are completely satisfied. The price you pay for a thing is what determines its value. If you had a Ferrari, you would not sell it for 20 pounds, because it is worth so much more to you. In the same way you would spend thousands of pounds to purchase it if you were the buyer, because you think it is worth the price. It is such a sad reality that people actually value items more than people, when God paid for us with the most precious thing heaven had to offer: Jesus Christ. Apostle Peter says this: "...You were not redeemed with corruptible things, like silver or gold, from your aimless conduct received by tradition from your fathers, but with the precious blood of Christ, as of a lamb without blemish and without spot" (I Peter☐ 1:18-19☐ NKJV☐☐). What you go for is the blood of Jesus. Your value is literally the blood of Jesus, because you are that important to the Father. When you know this, it becomes harder for you to sell yourself so that society can value you. It becomes harder for little Tyrone to shoplift because being bad is celebrated and valued among the friendship group, if he sees his value before the Father. It would have been easier for me to say no when I was tempted to lose my virginity. My value before the Father would have held greater weight than the devaluing worth of friends and society. Your

value is in the perfect love of the
Father. □□□□□□□□□□□□

Acceptance is found in the perfect love of God.

As previously mentioned, Paul reminds the
church at Ephesus that they were accepted in
the beloved. The sin that hung over us and made
us enemies of God in our minds has been nailed
to the cross of Christ and through our faith in
Him we have become friends with Him. We are
eternally accepted. Understanding the
acceptance of the Father gives power to your
Christianity because it means you don't mind
the rejection that is promised to believers from
the world. The reason for compromise is the
need for acceptance. You will not compromise to
fit into a particular friendship group in order to
be accepted, if you know you are accepted by
God. It is important to know that not only young
people struggle with this; adults do too. The
reason why many adults join in when gossip is
going on about a staff member at work is
because they want to feel accepted by
colleagues. I repeat you would not compromise

so easily if you knew you were accepted by God.

Security is also found in the perfect love of God. God is a Father that never changes. He is the same yesterday, today and forever. He will not accept you today and reject you tomorrow; that's against His nature and character. Many have fathers who have denied their responsibilities as fathers and rejected their children, and this often enables negative perception when it comes to seeing God as Father. But God is a perfect Father. He is the standard; natural fathers are not the standard and God never changes His mind.

I often advise people, especially young women, when they find a guy they like and are thinking about having a relationship with, that they should learn to love God first. The reason for this is that men are not immune to mistakes. Men are inconsistent; they can say yes today and no tomorrow, men can easily let you down; therefore you can't afford to place all of your security in them. I'm not saying don't trust them, but I'm saying bear in mind that you could get disappointed. True love knows the other may let them down, but they are willing to love regardless. God knows you may disobey Him tomorrow but He is still willing to love you, because His love is not self-seeking. If as a young woman, you look to a man for your security and he lets you down, you would be heartbroken. But if you look to the consistent Father who never changes and is incapable of letting you down, then you have your security. Security is found in the perfect love of the Father expressed through the cross of Christ.

Learning from the firstborn

It is amazing how the sacrifice of Jesus tells us so much about the Father. In fact the whole life of Jesus tells us about the Father, because one of His main missions was to reveal the Father and in doing so, bring glory to His name. It is important to understand that Jesus did not only come to die for the sins of man but to show God's purpose for man which is the life He modelled. So, how do I know how to live like a son? I open the scriptures and look at the life of Jesus. I become His disciple, a life-long learner, who learns His manner of life and doctrine. I make Him my example by acknowledging Him as God's firstborn Son.

The word "firstborn" in Greek means "first in time". This is where pre-eminence comes from. It means that Jesus is first in authority and, in fact, He is first to go through glorification. All of this is important for the crux of what I am explaining, which is that Christ is our pattern or example. Essentially Christ is our foundation and context for sonship. You live like a son when you follow the example of your older brother, Jesus Christ. It is important to know that through the death and resurrection of Jesus Christ, you are now His younger brother, which means you are a son of the Father. This is why He is not ashamed to call you brother (Hebrews 2:11 ESV). This is also why in John's gospel, after He resurrected, He told Mary Magdalene to tell His brothers that He was going to His Father, who is also their Father (John 20:17). The whole of the Christian life as well as manifesting sonship is looking and learning from the life and example of Jesus our big brother, the firstborn of the Father.

The author of Hebrews said that in the past, God

spoke to the fathers by the prophets, but in these last days, He has spoken to us through His Son. Of the Son, the author said, "Who being the brightness of His glory and the express image of His person..." (Hebrews 1:3 NKJV). We learn through the life of our older brother that the apex of sonship is being the brightness of the Father's glory. Brightness is the Greek word "pheggos", which translates to radiance or more accurately light. This is big because the work of light is to reveal or to manifest. Therefore, Christ is the revelation of God's glory, the manifestation of His intrinsic worth, nature and essence. The way He could be the revelation or manifestation of God's essence is by being the image of His person (character). God created the first Adam to be the manifestation of His essence, but the first Adam failed. However, the last Adam who was sent for that purpose prevailed. Being what we were created to be (sons) and doing what we were created to do (manifest the glory of God) are only made possible by following the example of Jesus Christ and rejecting the example of Adam. Apostle John encourages us to follow in the footsteps of Christ in his epistle by saying: "He who says he abides in Him ought himself also to walk just as He walked" (I John☐ 2:6☐ NKJV). JUST AS! The Apostle Paul goes as far as to say that the intent of God predestining and creating us was to conform us into the image of His Son (Romans 8:39). Following the example of Jesus isn't only an encouragement but the essence of our existence. Following the example of Adam and submitting to the devil are the ways to ruin this world.☐☐☐☐☐☐☐☐☐☐☐☐☐

John in his gospel, poetically taught us how Christ revealed the purpose of mankind. Let's explore a verse previously mentioned in the first chapter in greater detail.

In John 15:1 Jesus said, "I am the vine and my Father is the vinedresser." You don't have to see a gardener to know he is amazing; all you have to do is look at his garden. The garden is the workmanship of the gardener that reveals his skill; such is Christ to the Father. When you see the splendid work of the gardener, then you're likely to hire him to take care of your garden as well. As the gardener cultivates the garden, the Father dressed Christ and He dresses every one of His sons and daughters. The Father is the light, soil, and rain of the Son. Thus, the Son was able to reveal the Father. This teaches me that if I'm going to reveal my Father, then I'm going to have to let Him pour into me. I'm going to let Him prune me, (but let's save that for the chastising of sons). I'm going to have to let Him mould and shape me according to His will, so I can manifest Him.

In the fifth chapter of John, Jesus said, "Most assuredly, I say to you, the Son can do nothing of Himself, but what He sees the Father do; for whatever He does, the Son also does in like manner. For the Father loves the Son, and shows Him all things that He Himself does; and He will show Him greater works than these, that you may marvel" (John□ 5:19-20□ NKJV□).□ From the life and example of Jesus, we learn some key lessons about sonship which lead to the revelation of the Father's glory.□□□□□□□□□□□□□

• Sons are totally dependent on their Father.
• Sons are completely submissive to their Father.
• Sons are intimate (one) with their Father.
• Sons are imitators of their Father and His will.

- Sons never operate outside of the context of their Father.

This is sadly true for sons of the devil but gloriously true for sons of Abba Father. For the believer, sonship is deciding to know nothing and to be unable to do anything outside the Father and His will. So, there is complete dependence on the Father. The Father's truth becomes your truth, His way, your way and His life, your life. He is your source and you can't operate outside of His will, direction and order. He is also the power that works in and through you. This is why the spirit of sonship, which is the Holy Spirit, lives in sons of God. It is through the Holy Spirit that the Father works through the Son as well as His sons and daughters. This is where intimacy or oneness with God comes in, because the Holy Spirit was the middle man that communicated what the Father was doing and saying them to the Son, and so the Son was able to do the same thing. We must develop intimacy with the Holy Spirit, but we will explore this when we look at the 5th and 6th chapters.

It is important to know that Jesus chose to do nothing by Himself; He completely depended on God the Father. It shows that if we decide to make God our source and completely depend on Him and be completely submissive to Him, we will do what Jesus did and reveal the Father. The challenge of sonship is to see what the Father is doing in the heavenly realm and replicate it on earth; it is a challenge because it takes total surrender to the will, order and leading of God. If we do this, we would be imitators of God, doing what the Father does, saying what He says and being the brightness of His glory on earth as Christ was. We would be the garden revealing the gardener. Like Jesus, we would also be able to say, "When you've seen us, you've seen the Father." I would just like to emphasise that this takes total dependence, submission and intimacy with God. We must possess all these keys if we are to be sons manifesting our Father.

Do not trade your birthright

Jesus' example of living a life free of sin teaches us to guard our birthright. The author of Hebrews calls Esau foolish because he sold his birthright for a moment in the flesh to satisfy himself (Hebrews 12:16). We do the same every time we sin. As Christians, our birthright is the glory of God. Sons reveal their Father and bring glory to His name; it is our legal right. 'God is Spirit' as Jesus said to the woman at the well in (John 4:24) and as He said to Nicodemus (John 3:6) 'that which is born of the Spirit is spirit'. This means that our regeneration makes us spirit, enabling us to reveal that our Father is Spirit. It is utter foolishness to trade such a privilege for a moment of instant gratification in the flesh. Being spiritual beings, means that we are holy and set apart because our culture is not carnal and earthly but spiritual and heavenly. Thus, we are empowered to be ambassadors of God's kingdom, which is another birthright of sons.

When we sin we are not glorifying God. We are being carnal and not spiritual. It means that we are trading our birthright for a moment in the flesh. I repeat foolishness. Wisdom teaches us to value the glory of God and value our identity as conduits of the revelation of His nature and kingdom on earth. When we understand the price that God paid to redeem us into our original identity and birthright as spirits, it will cause us to guard it jealously. We will mute the voice of foolishness, which tells us to sin and trade it for a moment in the flesh.

I was on Facebook live one evening, and I heard this mind-blowing revelation from a man of God. I do believe it would help us to understand this issue of guarding our birthright. He said that when God created Adam, He created the spirit first in Genesis 1. This means that the spirit was the firstborn. Adam was first a spirit. But then in the 2nd chapter, God created the body: the flesh to contain the spirit on earth. The birthright belonged to the spirit just as the birthright belonged to Esau because he was the firstborn. However, when Adam rebelled, sin caused him to foolishly sell the birthright of the spirit to the flesh. Instead of the spirit having the biggest influence over man, the flesh started to have the biggest influence. Man went from being spiritual to being carnal. Now through the redemption of Christ Jesus, we are back to the position Adam was before the fall! "That which is born of Spirit is spirit!" The birthright of the spirit has been restored through regeneration. No longer are we carnal, but our flesh contains who we are, our spirit. Our spirit (who we are) now rule and govern our soul and flesh as Christ rules our spirit. When temptations come, we must not act foolishly and cast our birthright to the flesh and have it rule us.

Chapter 4: Sonship before Ministry

'We can't just become sons of God; we become sons of God through the work of God, the redemption of Christ and the filling of the Spirit of Sonship. Once our identity is established, then we, like Christ, qualify to be priests and worshippers of the living God.'

Chapter 4: Sonship before Ministry

All are ministers

Whether you are officially in ministry as a five-fold ministry gift (Apostle, Prophet, Evangelist or Teacher), a deacon, worship leader or whether you're not an official minister in that sense, you are still a minister of God as long as you are fulfilling your divine assignment and serving God in a relevant and fruitful capacity. A minister means a servant. However, it is absolutely vital that the context of ministry or service is sonship.

Being a minister of God does not always mean standing behind the pulpit preaching the gospel, or holding a microphone and leading worship. It doesn't always come with a title. However, it looks like washing the feet of those around you. It looks like giving yourself and laying down your life for the purposes of God. This in turn leads to you loving and serving God's creation. This is not contingent on a particular context. It doesn't matter if you are a teacher, student, banker, footballer or musician. You are a minister if you: serve God, those around you, and have laid down your life for them.

Sonship is the foundation of ministry

Jesus is an Apostle, Prophet, Evangelist and Teacher. However, He is most known and recognised as the Son of God. This tells us that the highest privilege of a believer is that in Christ they have become sons of God. Being sons of God speaks of our identity and being ministers speaks of our work. Our work must submit to the context of our identity. It means that we are to minister from the place of sonship or from our identity as sons of God.

A favourite preacher of mine called Todd White always said: "You do not do to be, but you be to do. Your doing has to come from a place of being." This means that you do not find yourself through the things that you do; however, what you do flows from who you are; your identity. Singing is sadly not one of my talents. It doesn't matter how many times I try to sing, it will not make me a singer. If I went on X-factor and the judges put me through to the stage past the audition, it would just be funny entertainment for the viewers. My point is this: singing doesn't make me a singer, as much as ministering and doing all the things you should do as a Christian make you a son of God. Living the Christian life is impossible when you try to work for acceptance. That is called performance-driven Christianity. The Jews in the Old Testament could not do it then and you can't do it now. In fact, before God, our own works and efforts are filthy rags. We must trust in the finished works of Christ and what He accomplished for us, and let our ministry flow from that place.

Your adoption is the work of the Father alone. You received it by faith and from receiving; you are empowered to minister, and not only minister, but to also reveal the Father through your ministry.

Our Elder brother Jesus, God's Firstborn, completely illustrates what ministry that is operating from sonship look like. It is interesting how before Jesus did any of His threefold ministry of preaching, teaching and healing, the

Father testified: 'This is my beloved Son in whom I am well pleased.' This happened after John baptised Him and the Holy Spirit came down in the bodily form and rested on Him. Jesus wasn't approved by God or accepted because He healed, taught and preached. In fact, He was approved as a Son before He went to the cross. He did His works and laid down His life from His identity as a Son approved by His Father. Sonship was first and thus was the foundation of His ministry. He preached, taught and healed as the Son of God and as your elder brother, Jesus Christ did, you also must minister as a son of God.

The author of Hebrews illustrated this in the third and fifth chapter of the book, and I'll show exactly how.

In the third verse of the third chapter of Hebrews, the author says that Jesus is worthy of much more honour than Moses for the builder of a house is worthy of more honour than the house he built. This means that the builder of Moses is actually Jesus because Jesus is God who built all things. The author then says in the 5th chapter that Moses was faithful in God's entire house as a servant and in the 6th chapter; he says that Christ was faithful as a Son. This tells us that sonship is greater than servanthood (ministry), because Christ who is worthy of greater honour was faithful as the Son. It's more glorious and honourable to be a son than a servant because sons reveal the Father, servants don't.

Even though Christ was a servant, He served as the Son, meaning His work or service revealed the Father. As Christians, we are both sons and servants. We cannot be one and not the other; we are both. Christ Himself was both. However, being a son is greater in the sense that it holds more weight literally and more kabod (glory). The foundation of all service and ministry must be sonship as previously discussed. The best way to be servants of God is through being sons of God. The role of a servant is to work, whilst the role of the son is to reveal the Father. If we serve God as sons then our work or service will glorify God because it will manifest the Father's nature.

In this specific context, the writer of Hebrews speaks of Christ's work as an Apostle, who is a builder. The builder of the house or church of God. Because Christ is the Son of God, the house He built and He is building in the earth is the revelation and reputation of the Father. This is true because God promised David in 2nd Samuel 7 that a seed is coming from him that will build a house for His name. Your name represents your identity, character and reputation. If you want to describe a well-known friend of yours to a person, you may say he is tall and describe his facial features, yet the person you are conversing with may be unsure about whom you are trying to describe. But once you mention your friend's name, he will know exactly who you are trying to describe. Then a smile will come upon the face of the person you are speaking to. Perhaps because the person you referred to is known in the church as well as the community and is an inspiration to loads of people. Do you see the power of the name? It gives you an identity. It speaks of your character and reputation. This is what Christ served to build for the Father: a house for His identity, character and reputation; a house that would reveal Him to the world.

He could only do such a work because He is the Son. His work revealed the Father because He worked from a place of sonship.

Besides, through the house the Son is building for the Father, the Father will vindicate His name and reputation. Christ served as the Son, building a house that will reveal the Father which is the church, whilst Moses was a servant to testify of what was to come. This also tells us that it doesn't take sons to tell people that Christ is returning. Servants can do that with microphones and leaflets. However, it takes sons to show the face of the Father to the world as Christ did, so that they would want to belong to the Father because of how amazingly His sons reveal Him. As sons of God, our job is not only to serve by preaching that Christ will return, but to reveal His nature and His character by housing His presence on the earth. We can only do this if we are sons. This means that as we tell people about Christ, we are also demonstrating His nature and character, so that through us the Father's house and His name can be a praise on the earth.

The point I'm making essentially is this, serving as a son means that your work will reveal the Father, whether you're in business, a pastor or a school teacher. Everything you do, if it flows from a place of sonship, will bring glory to the Father's name.

God is more interested in sons than servants

This is especially sobering if you take greater pride in your title or the work you do over your identity as a son of God. Jesus says this powerful, yet convicting phrase in Matthew 9:18: "I desire mercy not sacrifice." The context of this statement is that Jesus had just told Matthew the tax collector to follow Him. He was having dinner with Matthew and some tax collector friends not long after. The Pharisees then started to condemn Jesus and asked Him why He was eating with sinners and tax collectors. In biblical time and Jewish history, eating with someone is a proof that you have completely accepted them. This is why Jesus breaking bread with His disciples was so significant. After they questioned Jesus, His response was, "It's the sick that need a doctor and not the healthy. I have not come to call the righteous but sinners to repentance" (Mark 2:17). Then He told the Pharisees to go and learn what God meant when He spoke through the prophet Hosea that He 'desires mercy and not sacrifice.' What Jesus was teaching the Pharisees through this whole experience is that God is more interested in His nature and character being seen as opposed to pointless ritual and religious activities done in service (ministry) to Him.

Prophet Isaiah explained true and false fasting when he wrote, "Behold, you fast only to quarrel and to fight and to hit with a wicked fist. Fasting like yours this day will not make your voice to be heard on high. Is such the fast that I choose, a day for a person to humble himself? Is it to bow down his head like a reed, and to spread sackcloth and ashes under Him? Will you call this a fast and a day acceptable to the Lord?" (Isaiah☐ 58:4-5☐ ESV☐). Isaiah, the messianic prophet, also revealed the kind of fast that God approved of, "Is not this the fast that I choose: to lose the bonds of wickedness, to undo the straps of the yoke, to let the oppressed go free, and to break every yoke?" (Isaiah☐58:6☐ ESV☐☐).
☐☐☐☐☐☐☐☐☐☐☐☐☐☐☐☐☐☐☐☐☐☐☐☐☐☐☐☐☐☐☐☐☐☐☐
☐☐☐☐☐☐☐☐☐☐☐☐☐☐☐☐☐☐
God was unhappy about His people's service unto Him, which was fasting. He was unhappy

about their sacrifice and worship because it was doing nothing to reveal His character. It was all ministry but no sonship, no glory. There were contentions and strife amongst the people and there was no mercy upon the broken people around them. So their service, sacrifice and worship were useless. The reason God is more interested in sons than servants is because He is interested in the glory of His name. He is more interested in sons that will reveal His glory through the work that they are doing just as Christ did. Whenever Christ healed the sick, He was serving but those who were healed could see the Father through His ministering. They could see His love and compassion over their situation and the power He had to change it. The same thing can be said for when He multiplied five loaves and two fish to feed five thousand.

However, the Pharisees who esteemed themselves as ministers of God, rebuked Jesus whenever He healed on the Sabbath day. I would read through the 5th chapter of John and think what is wrong with these Pharisees? A man was born blind and had been in darkness all his life. Now he can finally see and all you can do is complain about the fact that he was healed on the Sabbath day. Aren't you happy that he's been healed from his condition? Where is your compassion? This is a typical example illustrating the reason why service or ministry must submit to the context and foundation of sonship.

An issue I dealt with and several people also deal with is finding themselves through the work that they do. I remember when the culture of healing and creative miracles broke out in my life. I fell into the danger of finding myself through the healing that occurred when I prayed for the sick. When two or three days passed without the occurrence of a physical healing through my prayers, I would begin to get very discontent. I would leave my house, looking for people to pray for and heal. That was not always because I cared about their pain, but because healing the sick made me feel important. This is ministry outside of the context of Sonship because its heart wasn't revealing God's nature. Whether you're a preacher, worship leader, gifted poet, artist, prophet, soul winner, fill in the blank, none of those things is what makes you important. It's the perfect love of the Father that makes you important. It's the fact that the

Father thought you were worth redeeming, even though you did nothing to deserve it and Jesus purchased you. If preaching makes you feel important, what if the doors to speaking engagements close? If it's singing, what if you never make it as a singer or what if you're no longer required on the worship team? If you're a poet, what if no one comes to your show? Are you no longer important? Have you lost all significance? No, because it doesn't change how the Father sees you. It doesn't change the truth of you being His son, the apple of His eyes, the one He rejoices over with singing (Zephaniah 3:17), the one whose strands of hair He has taken the time to number (Luke 12:7).

You have to remember that your worth is rooted in your identity as a son of God. This is a firm foundation. Nothing can change that because God the Father will never change His mind about you. One thing that is guaranteed is that God will never disown you. However, opportunities to manifest your gift may stop coming and people may not even appreciate your craft. Being found in gifting is what compels preachers to water down their message for those who have itching ears because they want to be approved and accepted by people;

they want people to like their preaching. Your acceptance and worth can be lost if they are not rooted in your sonship.

Vessels of wood and clay get used too

Finding yourself through ministry and not sonship will find you on the pages of Matthew 7:22. The problem with those who said they cast out devils in Jesus' name as well as prophesied and performed many miracles in His name is that they found themselves through what they were doing and they thought it was God's mark of approval over their lives. However, the truth is that vessels of wood and clay get used too. The Scripture affirms this, "But God's firm foundation stands, bearing this seal: "The Lord knows those who are His," and, "Let everyone who names the name of the Lord depart from iniquity." Now in a great house there are not only vessels of gold and silver but also of wood and clay, some for honourable use, some for dishonourable. Therefore, if anyone cleanses himself from what is dishonourable, he will be a vessel for honourable use, set apart as holy, useful to the master of the house, ready for

every good work" (2 Timothy 2:19-
21 ESV).

Paul, in his second letter to Timothy, told him
that there are different vessels in a house; some
of gold and silver and some of wood and clay. He
went on to tell Timothy to make sure he
cleanses himself from the latter. The key thing
about this verse is that all vessels are going to be
used, even the wood and clay. Therefore, God
using you is not the goal. Being a minister or
servant is not the goal. The fact that God is using
you is not God's stamp of approval on your life.
You can't find yourself through your
ministering.

Your stamp of approval is that you name the
name of Jesus and you have departed from
iniquity. When you have a son or a daughter, he
or she will be given your family name and if you
are a parent, your child already has your name.
Your relationship with God is what approves
you. It is the fact that you're His son and you
bear His name. You are one with Him; therefore,
you've departed from iniquity because there is
no iniquity in the one you are now one with.
Being in an intimate relationship with God, as
His son, is your mark of approval, not the things

that He does through you. The people Jesus referred to in Matthew 7:22 said they performed miracles, prophesied and cast out devils, but none of them said they were God's son.

The foundation for worship is sonship

The Scripture expressly says, "So also Christ did not exalt Himself to be made a high priest, but was appointed by Him who said to Him, "You are my Son, today I have begotten you"; as he says also in another place, "You are a priest forever, after the order of Melchizedek" (Hebrews 5:5-6 ESV).

The author was incredibly deliberate in Christ being affirmed as Son first before His affirmation as a priest. As Christ was affirmed as a priest, we are also affirmed as a royal priesthood. As we have learnt, Christ is the standard of sonship, so His process paves the way for our process. If His sonship fuelled His priesthood, our sonship must also fuel our priesthood. The importance of this is this: The one who qualifies us to be sons is also the one who qualifies us to be priests (worshippers and ministers). We cannot just become sons of God; we become sons of God through the work of God, the redemption of Christ and the infilling of the Spirit of sonship. Once our identity is established, then we, like Christ, qualify to be priests and worshippers of the living God. Our identity as sons and worshippers cannot puff us up because we never earned it. It was freely given to us by the Father; therefore it brings great humility to us. We understand that all good things we can receive and have received are from the Father and they keep us dependent on Him.

Sonship is the foundation of priesthood because we worship from the place of being sons and not slaves. Slaves are obligated to be obedient to their masters, whether they love their masters or not, whether they think he/she is good or not. However, God will not accept any form of obedience that's not fuelled by love for Him. The greatest commandment is to love Him. Our worship and service to God must be fuelled by our love for Him. We love Him because He first loved us (1 John 4:19) and His love is expressed in that He made us His sons. "See what kind of love the Father has given to us, that we should

be called children of
God" (1 John☐ 3:1☐ ESV☐☐). If you don't see
that you are His child, then it will be hard for
you to love Him, because it means you haven't
truly seen or received His love. This is how to
make God seem like a tyrannical slave master
and you a religious, joyless servant. Because
sonship is the foundation of our worship, our
submissions and obedience are fuelled by love
for Him. This is why John 14:15 says, "If we love
Him, we will obey His commandments." We are
not slaves begrudgingly doing the will of our
master. We are sons joyfully and lovingly
fulfilling the purposes of our Father. The
relationship between sonship and priesthood
will be further explored when we look
at "Sonship, Worship and the Presence of
God" in the 5th chapter.

Chapter 5: Sonship and the Presence of God

'God's sons are carriers of His presence and His glory. They have His indwelling presence, abiding presence and empowering presence. This is the secret of their exploits, and they will not trade their Father's presence for anything else in the world.'

Chapter 5: Sonship and the Presence of God

Freedom is in the presence of God

There is an amazing parallel to draw between Adam and Jesus on one hand and Ishmael and Isaac on the other, when we speak about sonship. Adam represents fallen humanity (slavery) and Jesus represents redeemed humanity (sonship). In a similar way, Hagar's son (Ishmael) represents the Jerusalem on earth, which is in slavery, whilst Isaac the son of Sarah represents the Jerusalem above, which is free (Gal. 4). I find it very interesting that God commanded Abraham to sacrifice his only son (Genesis 22), when Abraham had two sons. What's strikingly similar to this is that Jesus is recognised as the only Son of God (John 3:16) yet Adam is also recognised as the son of God in

Luke's account of the genealogy of Christ. God the Father and Abraham had two sons and only one of them is recognised as legitimate sons of their fathers. We learnt in the second chapter that Adam's disobedience to the word of God led to slavery. What Adam and Ishmael have in common is that they were both cast out of their father's presence. Ishmael and Hagar left the home of Abraham and Adam was cast out of Eden. The result of this was slavery. Slavery is the result when you are not in the presence of God. You become a slave to sin, a slave to the enemy, a slave to yourself, a slave to the opinions of man and society. Freedom can only be found in the presence of God.

In order to understand the presence of God, we have to understand, priesthood and worship. In the Old Testament, after Adam sinned, God's presence was no longer dwelling with and in man, until the time of Moses. God commanded Moses to build the ark of covenant (Exodus 25). The ark of covenant would house God's presence on earth so that He can dwell with His people. The ark is a type of Jesus and the new man that would come from Him (the church). David purposed in his heart to build a house for the name of the Lord. However, God promised him that his son will build the house. So, Solomon built a physical temple for the presence of God. However, he was a type and shadow of Christ who will build the spiritual dwelling of God on earth, which is the church. Now the temple had three parts: the outer court, inner court (holy place) and the Holy of holies. The book of Hebrews helps us to understand the way things operated under the Old Covenant. It says, "But only the high priest entered the inner room, and that only once a year, and never without blood, which he offered for himself and for the sins the people had committed in ignorance" (Hebrews 9:7 NIV)☐☐☐☐☐☐☐☐☐☐☐☐☐☐☐☐☐☐☐☐☐.

The way into the Holy of holies where God's presence dwelt had not yet come. The Scripture affirms it this way, "The Holy Spirit was showing by this that the way into the Most Holy Place had not yet been disclosed as long as the first tabernacle was still functioning" (Hebrews 9:8 NIV☐☐). ☐☐☐☐☐☐☐☐☐☐☐☐☐☐☐
Under the Old Covenant, the sons of Levi had the greatest privilege because they served as the

Levitical priests which means they were the ministers of the presence of God. The worshippers who rendered sacrifices to God came from their lineage. During those times, you could not even come close to the presence of God unless you were a high priest of the descent of Levi. That was because the priests were imperfect themselves; they would have to offer sacrifices for their sins and the sins of the people. Priests are intercessors and mediators on behalf of men to God, but the way into the Holy of holies changed after the rise of a new priest, the way into the most holy place will be bought by the sacrifice of this new priest who is the mediator of the new and better covenant, Jesus Christ. The author of Hebrews says this:

Hebrews☐ 9:11-14☐ NIV

But when Christ came as high priest of the good things that are now already here, he went through the greater and more perfect tabernacle that is not made with human hands, that is to say, is not a part of this creation. He did not enter by means of the blood of goats and calves; but he entered the Most Holy Place once for all by his own blood, thus obtaining eternal

redemption. The blood of goats and bulls and the ashes of a heifer sprinkled on those who are ceremonially unclean sanctify them so that they are outwardly clean. How much more, then, will the blood of Christ, who through the eternal Spirit offered himself unblemished to God, cleanse our consciences from acts that lead to death, so that we may serve the living God!

The blood of bulls and goats could only purify momentarily but the blood of Christ perfects us (saints) who believe forever. It purchased for us a new home, the presence of God. If the absence of God's presence brings slavery, the presence of God activates the life of a son and brings freedom. The Scripture says, "Because you are his sons, God sent the Spirit of his Son into our hearts, the Spirit who calls out, "Abba, Father." So you are no longer a slave, but God's child; and since you are his child, God has made you also an heir" (Galatians 4:6-7 NIV). What activates the presence of God is the Spirit of God. He is the breath and the life of God. Paul tells us in the second letter he wrote to the church at

Corinth that where the Spirit of the Lord is there is liberty. So, through God's breath, His presence is active in our lives and this results in our freedom. Remember God breathed into Adam and he became a living being. Everything Adam needed to be a son that reveals the Father was in that breath, and when he sinned the life of the Father in Adam vanished. However, in John's account of the resurrection of Jesus Christ, he testified that Jesus breathed into His disciples and said to them□□□□□□□□□□□□□, "Receive the Holy Spirit" (John 20:22). The presence of God that man lost was now restored through the death and resurrection of Christ.

Asaph's discovery in the sanctuary of the Lord

I want us to consider the story of Asaph in Psalm 73. This will help us to understand the purifying power of God's presence. But before we do, I want to show you something that occurred when Moses was leading the Israelites through the wilderness. This will enhance your understanding of the purifying power of God's presence.

When we explore Exodus 20 and we get to the 18th verse, we see that the children of Israel saw flashes of lightning and thundering and were terrified by the presence of God. They asked Moses to go and speak with God. They said they would rather listen to Moses than talk to God and die. Moses tried to encourage them to enter God's presence; he said that God had come to prove them and to put His fear before their faces so that they may sin no more. But they stood afar off, whilst Moses entered into the thick darkness. What happens when one neglects the presence of God is that he/she chooses to go without God's fear before their face and thus, chooses to keep their sin alive.

The answer to any issue of rebellion and disobedience against the will of God is the presence of God. It is entering into His presence and having His fear before your face that will kill your sin. The fear of the Lord is the foundation of the wisdom that will teach you to flee from evil and pursue righteousness. The fear of the Lord is found in the presence of God.

We can now explore how this played out in Asaph's life. I will encourage you to read Psalm 73 at this point, and then continue to read the book.

If you have read the psalm, you will see that you either are or have been Asaph. I know I have! Asaph considered the godless, prideful and lofty who prospered even though they were not worshippers of God. Then he asked himself if he has chastised and consecrated himself to God in vain. I remember after my repentance, I would see peers I used to hang out with at university, at clubs getting drunk and I used to envy them. I also remember when I used to idolise celebrities who were godless but had fame and fortune and so I wanted to be like them.

The seventeenth verse in this chapter is easily one of the most important verses in the Bible to me. It says: "Until I entered into the sanctuary of the Lord." This teaches us that perspective is aligned to wisdom in the presence of God! The presence of God imparts the fear of the Lord, and in turn imparts wisdom to sons. He realised that the prideful and their prosperity will become desolate in a moment. He realised his carnality and foolishness before the Lord. His words were: "I was brutish and ignorant; I was as a beast before you (verse 22)." Can you see how the fruit of neglecting the presence of God is earthly, unspiritual and demonic wisdom? It is sheer carnality, a sinful mindset that leads to a sinful lifestyle. This is what negligence to the presence of God will do in your life.

When he entered the presence of God, Asaph also made a discovery that I believe is THE MOST important discovery any human being can make. This is the discovery: the presence of God is his only need and desire. This is where true holiness comes from. His words were: 'Whom have I in heaven but you, and there is none that I desire on earth apart from you (verse 25).' In other words, the only reason I want to go to heaven is because you are there, and all I really want on earth is for you to be with me. Do you see the difference the presence makes? Because he entered into God's sanctuary, God's fear was before him and it produced wisdom. Wisdom caused him to desire God and God alone.

There is just something about God's presence! It frees us from the need to be satisfied by anything apart from God Himself. The issue of sin is the issue of satisfaction. It was Eric Gilmour that said this: "That which you go to for satisfaction is that which you worship." All the while, Jesus has called those who thirst to Himself. He also promised that He would give them water, and out of their bellies will come forth rivers of living waters (John 7:37). We know that the water He spoke of was the Holy Spirit, who is the presence of God. Those who come to the presence, for the presence, will leave satisfied to the point that they are overflowing with God's presence. Those who neglect His presence or only come to Him for presents will want; this will create desire for satisfaction which often leads to sin.

It is possible to drink from the flowing rivers of life but then trade Him for broken cisterns that hold no water. Israel did it in the time of the prophet Jeremiah and Christians do it today. I have found to be true in my own life, that when I neglect the presence of God, or when something else takes a higher place in the throne of my heart, ungodly desires erupt in my soul. My solution is to make His presence my greatest desire again. This happens when I come to Him and drink as it did when Asaph entered the sanctuary. We Christians must realise that coming to drink on a weekly basis will not suffice; we must come to Him daily and all our needs for satisfaction will be met. Eric Gilmour also said this: "Satisfaction isn't simply a perk of His presence, it's the very means through which He frees us and empowers us, to be able to obey Him." We are freed from disobedience and empowered for obedience in and by the presence of God. Holiness, which is a mark of sons, is the fruit of a life that is lived in the presence of God.

We must bare this in mind: The one promising us satisfaction when we come to Him is the one who multiplied five loaves and two fish to feed five thousand hungry men. After they filled their bellies, there were twelve baskets leftover. We need not question the integrity of His promise, or His ability to provide even beyond our point of satisfaction.

When Jesus spoke about those who will have their part in hell, He started the list with 'the fearful' (Revelation 21:8). Did it shock you? It shocked me too upon my first glance. However, it started to make sense when I remembered the children of Israel, who were too fearful to enter into God's presence and neglected Him. Then I learnt that Jesus started this list with cowards because it is the well through which every other sinful desire and action flows from. Running away from the presence of God because of your sin or temptation is the wrong move! Being too fearful, to come before God's presence will keep your sin alive. Your sin can only die when you live in the presence of God.

How to engage with God's presence

Matthew☐ 6:6☐ (NKJV☐☐)

But you, when you pray, go into your room, and when you have shut your door, pray to your Father who is in the secret place; and your Father who sees in secret will reward you openly.

When Jesus taught His disciples to pray, He taught them that the most vital things for a vibrant prayer life are: solitary and quietness. The prayer closet or being alone in your room helps you to find solitude and quietness so that you can give all your attention to God. It is important to know that the secret place is not your room. The secret place is God's dwelling place. It is the spiritual, heavenly realm. When you come to God in faith through the access Jesus gives you to God's presence, and you've found solitude and quietness, you can access God easily because He has all your attention. When you have solitude, quietness and God has all your attention then begin to pray and worship. Your room or prayer closet gives you external solitude and quietness; however the goal of the son is to find solitude and quietness internally, in their soul. The beauty of this is that you are able to access the secret place on your way to the mall, on the street, at work and even at school. I can be in a room full of people but access the secret place when my soul finds solitude and quietness with God and He has all my attention. This is how to enter into the secret place, no matter where you are. But understand this; you have to crawl before you walk. So make sure you have established a culture of getting into the prayer closet, and never graduate from it! This is what will train you to access the secret place wherever you go. The easier you find external solitude and quietness when communing with God, the easier you will find internal solitude and quietness.

The next time you pray or worship, find solitude and quietness and then give Him all your attention. What you then need to do is come to God with the awareness of your need for Him. These are the words of David: "God you are my God, earnestly I seek you, my soul thirsts for you, my flesh faints for you as in a dry and weary land where there no water" (Psalm 63:1 ESV).

When we read this from the bottom up, we see the progression. It starts with **dependency.**

David likened himself to a desert without moisture. David teaches us that it starts with being poor in spirit. He realised that he was in need of satisfaction but then went to God for satisfaction. David knew that as water would satisfy a dry land, God would satisfy him. His dependency gave birth to **desire**.

 I have found to be true in my own life, that the most blissful times in the presence of God are the times where I have approached God with an awareness of my need for Him; my utter brokenness apart from Him. This has created desire and hunger to be with Him, which causes me to **seek** Him in a way that erupts from my heart as worship and adoration. It causes me to see Him in a way that exalts him to be the beautiful and awesome God that He truly is. Naturally when your body tells you that you need food, you get hungry and you start to desire it. In the same way, your heart will be hungry when it sees its need for God. From dependency, David became hungry, his soul literally began to desire God and his desire caused him to seek God.

If a person is not fasting and he tells me he is starving and has a fridge full of food in his kitchen, which he can easily access, but just chooses not to eat, I'm sorry, he is not starving. The starvation will cause him to get to the fridge and make himself something to eat. The truth is God is not God to those who don't seek Him, because those who don't seek Him are not hungry for Him. Those who are not hungry for Him do not realise their need for Him.

Dependency breeds desire which breeds seeking. To seek for something or someone is to look for that thing. It's for that thing to have all your attention. Worship is simply turning your attention towards God, being after his heart. It is beholding His face. God promised to reward those who seek Him diligently. As you seek Him, expect Him and He will reward you with Himself. God is love, joy, peace, rest, strength, power, wisdom, kindness, goodness, and more. He will reward you with the facet of Himself that He feels you need most in the moment, when you seek Him.

Just take a look at this verse for a minute, read it twice! **"In the days of His flesh, Jesus offered up prayers and supplications, with loud cries and tears, to Him who was able to save Him from death, and He was heard because of His reverence." (Hebrews 5:7 ESV)**

The keys we find in David's life that made his prayer and worship life successful, are the same keys we find in our elder brother, Jesus. He knew God the Father was the one who was able to save Him from death. The awareness of His need for His Heavenly Father created dependency for the presence of His Heavenly Father. Why do you think He often turned people away to be alone with Abba? Dependency in turn created desire, and desire caused him to seek God the Father intensely, to the point of tears and loud cries!

Prayer is a form of worship (seeking) because the heart of prayer is dependency and desire. It is your dependency and desire that makes you a worshipper. It is what makes you a seeker. His need for the presence of God caused Him to hunger for the presence of God and seek the presence of God. What this revealed about Jesus was also what caused His prayer to be heard: His reverence; His godly fear. You know who truly fears God by who truly depends upon His presence to live. The fear of God is realising that God's presence is the only thing that can keep you alive. It causes you to cleave to God. The thought of being apart from Him is terror to your soul, because you know it results in death. JESUS KNEW THAT GOD THE FATHER WAS THE ONE WHO WAS ABLE TO SAVE HIM FROM DEATH! The one who doesn't fear God will not pray or worship. They will not seek God because they do not think they need Him to live. What we learn from David is what we learn from Jesus: depend, desire and seek, and the result is life. This is how sons engage with their Heavenly Father. This is how intimacy is created. Without engaging with God's presence in this way, you will be a son only in theory. Theoretical sons cannot display the life of the Father.

There's a very simple and practical way to put depending, desiring and seeking into action. Put the book down, find solitary and quietness, give God all your attention and simply say: "GOD, I need you, I desire you, I worship (seek) you, with all my heart I seek you, you deserve all my attention...." now continue, take as long as you need.

Sons have the licence to draw close

Many think that John was the disciple Jesus loved the most, because John called himself the one whom Jesus loved. However, this can't be true. Jesus came to reveal the Father and the Father does not love one child more than the other. This is the truth of the matter: John knew he was loved by Jesus and that was what beckoned him to get close to the Lord. In the thirteenth chapter of John's Gospel, after Jesus had washed His disciples' feet, He was having dinner with them and then He mentioned that one of them was going to betray Him. Whilst this was going on, John was sitting very close to Jesus; he even had his head on His bosom, and Peter asked John to ask Jesus who the person that would betray Him was. It is always the ones afar that ask the ones who are close to inquire of the lord. What differentiates the one afar and the one who is close is their understanding of God's love for them. Jesus told John that He would dip the bread and give it to the person that would betray. This is exactly what happened. John knew and understood the love Christ had for him, which gave him the access to draw close to Christ. It also positioned him to receive secrets and revelation from Jesus. As sons, completed and accepted by the Father, and recipients of His lavish love, we have access to draw close to His side as well as to receive insight and revelation from Him. John's gospel says this: "No one has seen God at any time. The only begotten Son, who is in the bosom of the Father, He has declared Him" (John☐ 1:18☐ NKJV☐☐).

This is key because it's God's firstborn Son, Jesus, our elder brother who was able to make God known because He is at the Father's side. Just as John was at Jesus' side, Jesus was at the Father's side. I don't think it is coincidental that the revelation of Jesus Christ came from John. The son, who is by the side of God
(in God's presence), is the one who is empowered to make Him known.

In God's presence is the power that conforms you to His person.

I once heard a preacher, Dr Matthew Stevenson, make this statement: "In the presence is the power that conforms you to His person." This statement has stayed with me ever since. This is the truth because when we explore the word "presence" in the Hebrew, we see that it is the word "panim" or "paneh", which translates to face or faces. Paul, in his second letter to the church at Corinth, said: "And we all, with unveiled face, beholding the glory of the Lord, are being transformed into the same image from one degree of glory to another. For this comes from the Lord who is the Spirit" (2 Corinthians 3:18 ESV).

This means whenever we are in the presence of God, fellowshipping with the Holy Spirit in word, prayer, worship or just simply meditating on His goodness in our minds, we are beholding His face. This is the spiritual reality. The veil is lifted from our hearts and through salvation; God has purified our hearts so that we can see Him. As we spend time in His presence, the Holy Spirit reveals Christ (the manifest presence and face of God) and conforms us to the image we are beholding so that His presence and face can be manifested through our lives. The life of a son is simply this, behold the Father's face in secret and be an open display of it. The presence of God empowers us to be what we've been created to be - sons of God. Upon his persecution, Stephen beheld god's glory and instantly conformed into the image of Christ. As Christ forgave his persecutors, Stephen forgave his persecutors. It was as long as Peter could behold God's glory (Jesus) that he could conform to the likeness of Christ and walk on water. When he stopped beholding he lost his ability to conform and walk like Christ.

Furthermore, in his letter to the church at Ephesus, Paul said that we have been blessed with every spiritual blessing in heavenly places. It is important to understand what our spiritual blessings are and where they are located. Those blessings, I believe, are all the things that make it possible to display the character of God and bring glory to His name. So they include His character, wisdom and power. But these blessings are located in the spirit; they don't have a physical location. Jesus, in the fourth chapter of John's gospel, told the Samaritan woman that the Father is looking for worshippers who will worship Him in spirit and in truth. The spirit is a location where we meet with God to worship Him. Let me reiterate that according to Psalm 91, the secret place is not your room; it is the secret place of the most high; it is God's dwelling place, and God dwells in the spirit. Therefore, we worship God in spirit, in the heavenly places and as we do, He endows us with virtues (spiritual blessings) that enable us to manifest His character and reveal His nature on earth.

Sons are the expression of their Father's presence (Ambassadors of the Kingdom of

God)

Jesus' name is Immanuel, meaning God with us. This means Jesus personified the presence of God. When Jesus is in an environment God is there also. During His earthly ministry, when Jesus was with people, God was also with those people. And a lot of times, this looked like the occurrence of healings and miracles because it was the presence of God that made them happen. We will explore what this looks like with the testimonies in the next chapter.

In the sixth chapter of Matthew, Jesus told His disciples to pray that God's kingdom will come and His will be done on earth as it is in heaven. God never lost sight of the reason He created Adam. His oneness with Adam would mean oneness between heaven and earth, and His sons would be the conduits of this reality. Heaven is the realm of the fullness of God's presence. It is also the perfect illustration of God's kingdom because everything submits to His will in that realm.

Paul says the kingdom of God is neither meat

nor drink, but is righteousness peace and joy in the Holy Spirit. This means that the kingdom of God is in the domain of the Spirit. This tells us that the Holy Spirit (God's presence) freely dwells in realms, areas and people that are submitted to God. We welcome more of God's Spirit and presence in our lives by our level of surrender and submission to His will. The Spirit then produces righteousness peace and joy. One of the commodities of the kingdom of God is righteousness. This is because there is no sin in realms that are wholly submitted to God. In the same way, it would be hard to spot sin in the life of one who is completely submitted to God, hence why we can't identify sin in the life of Christ. The second commodity is peace. The atmosphere of the kingdom of God is peace. There is no chaos or torment, just wholeness and liberty which brings about peace.

Christ slept in a boat and walked on water in the midst of storms because His external circumstance could not overwhelm the reality of the kingdom and presence of God in His spirit. Christ was full of contentment and joy, although no one has ever suffered to the extent that He did in the whole of human race.

Hebrews 2 states that He was anointed with the oil of gladness. Christ, the Son of God, was the expression of the kingdom of God. His life was a life of righteousness, peace and joy. Because of this, He was an ambassador of the kingdom of God.

The presence of God made possible in His life what it made possible in the realm of God's kingdom; Christ was literally heaven on earth. The same Christ tells us that the kingdom is within us and it makes sense that the kingdom is within us because the Holy Spirit dwells in our hearts. The kingdom is in the Holy Spirit. If we should submit to God as Christ did, we would activate this realm to greater capacities in our lives and like Christ, we too will become ambassadors of the kingdom of God, living illustrations of what it looks like. We would practice righteousness and earthly circumstance will not be able to take our peace and joy. In fact, we would overwhelm the earth with the reality of heaven, and watch heaven and earth become one through our lives.

The price Christ paid to give us the presence

When we neglect the presence of God, when we go without time with the Holy Spirit, when we fail to acknowledge and behold God, it does not only show our lack of desire and need for God, it also shows that we either don't understand or value the price Christ paid to make God's presence available to us. Through Christ we have confidence to enter the Holy of holies (Hebrews 10:19). Before Christ came and died, nobody could enter the Holy of holies. Not even the high priests I just need to re-emphasise this. Christ died to give you access to God's presence.

Remember the words of Christ, when He hung on the cross? "My God, My God why have you forsaken me?" Please let the weight of this hit your soul. The Son of God who continually referred to God as Father was without His Father momentarily, in order to make us sons. Again, He became what we were to make us what He is! He did not say, "My Father, why have you forsaken me?" He said, "My God." The truth is whilst He hung on the cross He did not feel like a son, He felt like an orphan, but we must ask why? Why did He feel like an orphan? He felt like an orphan because God's presence is what testifies about the sonship of an individual (Romans 8:16). Jesus said, "My God, why have you forsaken me?" To forsake is to abandon! The One, who has lived in and enjoyed the presence of the Father since eternity past and on earth, momentarily knew the feeling of being without His Father, in order to make you a son! He gave His life to make you a son who can access the presence of God forever!

When Jesus said, "I am thirsty," (John 19:28), what do you think He was thirsty for? We miss the whole point if we think that His thirst was purely physical. There definitely must have been an element of physical thirst: carrying the cross through Golgotha, all the blood that He lost and all the physical pain He felt would have made Him tired and thirsty. However, His thirst was not purely physical. There was a deeper thirst. We must remember that His suffering was not only physical. His deeper spiritual thirst came from being separated from His source of fulfilment and satisfaction: the all satisfying presence of the Father. Jesus was separated from the Father and the separation made Him thirsty because of our sin.

He sacrificed so much to make God's presence available to you! To neglect God's presence is to devalue and undermine His sacrifice and make it pointless. It's also to forfeit your ability to be a son of God. God sacrificed so much to give you His presence because of the value He attaches to His glory and your joy! In the presence of God, there is fullness of joy and at His right hand pleasures forevermore (Psalm 16:11). Without God's presence, it is impossible to fulfil the purpose of a son which is to glorify the Father. It is also impossible to experience the deepest and the most enduring kind of joy. Without God's presence, you settle for being a conceptual son, who has all the language without the practice.

I don't want you to feel condemned if you have been neglecting the presence of God. I am just trying to help you see how valuable He is to you. Your intimacy with God is valuable to you for your joy, identity and purpose and to God for His glory. Remember, the price you pay for a thing determines its value. Christ paid such a huge price. There is no way to fulfil the purpose of your existence without being with God. It is impossible to glorify God apart from God; so get into the secret place, abide in His presence and be who you've been created to be.

Chapter 6: The Works of Sons (Destroying the Works of the Devil)

'The key to fulfilling the great commission is evangelism. The ultimate goal of evangelism is to destroy the works of the devil.'

Chapter 6: The Works of Sons (Destroying the Works of the Devil)

Before you read this chapter, please consider the intentionality of the Holy Spirit to lead me to write the previous chapter before writing this one. We fall into a pit of the enemy if we bypass the presence of God and start working the works of sons. We position ourselves to be tired and burnt out if we do.

The works of sons is supposed to flow from their intimacy with the Father, and intimacy with the Father is cultivated through being in the presence of the Father. Before Jesus sent out His apostles to: preach, heal and deliver, He called them to Himself to first be with Him, and then He sent them out (Mark 3:14). He always says "come", before He says "go". He says this, so that His presence will be your empowerment to work the works of sons: The works that reveal the glory of the Father and destroy the works of the devil.

Upon the ascension of Christ, Jesus told the apostles to wait for the Holy Spirit to come upon them in Jerusalem, and they heeded Him (Acts 1). They did no ministry before they encountered God's presence. The coming of the presence of the Spirit upon them was what began and empowered their ministry. What we learn from Jesus telling them to tarry is one the most powerful things I've ever heard a preacher say: "God is most impressed with what He does Himself." You see the truth in this when you remember that the best of your deeds, in and of yourself, are filthy rags before Him.

Christianity is all about being, leave all the doing to the Holy Spirit. Leave all the doing to the presence of God. Jesus models utter dependency upon the presence of the Father for life and ministry when He said this: "It is the Father who abides in me that does the work", (John 14:10) essentially saying that He does nothing. However, the presence of the Father (Holy Spirit) is the one who works through Him. So sons must take a page out of the Son's book and learn to depend upon the presence of the Father for life and ministry. Prophet Isaiah first encountered God's manifest presence before he was purified by the seraph that touched his mouth with burnt coal, before he was sent out to preach (Isaiah 6).

Therefore, what we must learn to do is to cultivate the presence of God in our lives. We do this through having sweet communion with the Holy Spirit. We do this by realising our need for Him, desiring Him and rendering up adoration and worship towards Him. We do this by seeking Him, as communicated in the previous chapter. God's accommodation of choice is worship. As the psalmist says, "Yet you are the holy one enthroned on the praises of Israel" (Psalm 22:3 ESV). As we worship, we create an environment for His presence and dominion in our lives and on the earth. We create heaven on earth. This is the foundation and empowerment for working the works of sons and destroying the works of the devil.

Sonship and Evangelism

One of the works of the devil is to create a division between man and God through sin. In the context of Adam and Eve and all that were born into them, the enemy's work was successful. However, the Son of God, Jesus Christ, was made manifest to destroy the works of the devil (1 John 3:8) and reconcile man back to God (2 Cor. 5:18). In the same way, one of the fruits of our sonship is that the works of the devil is being destroyed through our lives. Another fruit of our sonship is that we are reconciling people back to God. One of the ways in which sons destroy the works of the devil is through evangelism. Note that I didn't say evangelists; I said sons; whether you're an evangelist or not, if you love God and people, you will evangelise and destroy the works of the devil. The book of Proverbs says this: "Rescue those who are being taken away to death; hold back those who are stumbling to the slaughter" (Proverbs☐ 24:11☐ ESV☐☐☐☐☐☐☐ ☐☐☐☐☐☐☐☐).

We do this by preaching the gospel and

manifesting the kingdom and presence of our Father. In doing so, we destroy the works of the devil by leading those who are headed for eternal damnation back into Eden, back into the presence of God as Christ, our older brother, did for us. If we fail to reach out and preach the gospel, we would allow people to enter into their death!

Knowing your identity fuels boldness for evangelism

One of the most frequently asked questions I hear from Christians is this, "Where does the boldness for evangelism come from?" People have often said this to me, "I want to preach the gospel. I want to tell people about Jesus, but when it comes to doing it, I get scared and I just choke, help!" I find it funny when people ask me this because I can completely relate to them. I remember one particular occasion, months after I began my journey with Christ and the burden for evangelism was upon my heart. I was on a train going to a friend's house and there was a young lady sitting at the seat in front of me. The thought to tell about Jesus came to me; somehow it came with the increase of my heart rate. The beat of my heart got louder; I got extremely fearful. Now that I think about it, it was crazy how scared and anxious I got. You would think a burglar had a gun to my head. Somehow, I mustered up the courage to tell her that Jesus loves her. It turned out she was a Christian, phew! After speaking to her the feeling was probably what David felt after slaying Goliath. I felt on top of the world.

Okay, let's fast forward to a couple of years after that experience. I was evangelising with a group of friends in Coventry England, boldly proclaiming the gospel to everyone I approached. A bunch of university students were waiting in line to enter into a club and I began to declare God's love to them, without any fear of persecution. One of the things that happened specifically during the outreach was I heard from the Lord that a particular boy had a leg that was a few inches shorter than the other.

This meant that this boy was always more slanted to one side and it strained his back. I approached him and asked if this was the case, after my partner Nia-Cerise called me over. She was speaking to him earlier on and planting seeds. He said, "Yes, I've always known it." Then I told him to get ready to see a miracle. God literally grew his leg and levelled it out with the other one. He had no words after the creative miracle occurred. I shared my testimony about how God saved me in my first year of university. I preached the gospel to him, and he decided to repent from his sins and surrender his life to Christ.

What shifted in two years? What was the difference between the young man who the thought of sharing Christ petrified and the young man who was boldly proclaiming the gospel, hearing from God, performing creative miracles and seeing souls come to Christ? The difference is a revelation on identity, understanding who I am as a son of God. Time with God is crucial! It was through a time of consecration and deeply seeking the presence of God that God spoke to me and affirmed me that I'm His son. Bill Johnson said this, "I can give you testimonies, but I can't give you personally history with God." It's a relationship! All believers must be able to point to a time when God spoke to them or did something that marked them forever.

When God revealed my identity as His son to me, I was studying the book of John, and I saw that Jesus called His disciples His brothers. I saw that throughout the Gospel of John, He would refer to Abba as my Father. But after He resurrected, He instructed Mary Magdalene to tell His brothers (disciples) that He was going to His Father who is their Father and His God who is their God. This made sense in my spirit. My heart connected with the truth of God (Abba) being Father and Jesus being my older brother for the first time. My earthly older brothers have always been examples in my life. Two people I look up to as role models. So, it was extremely easy for me to relate to Christ in that light. This changed everything. I have a Father who has accepted me, who loves me, who will never reject me. This truth is where the boldness to evangelise comes from.

The Bible is very clear that the message of the

cross is foolishness to those who are perishing (1 Corinthians 1:18). Jesus promised His disciples hatred from the world (John 15:18). As human beings, who want to be accepted and loved by people and who don't want to come across as foolish, who care so much about reputation, preaching the gospel to unbelievers is tasking. But when we understand that we are sons of God, loved by a perfect Father, accepted in the beloved, then we will willingly become foolish to the world because what our Heavenly Father thinks of us matters more.

Paul prayed a powerful prayer for the church at Ephesus. He prayed that the Ephesians (and all believers today) would know the heights, length, breadth and depth of God's love which surpasses knowledge and that they would be filled with the fullness of God. This tells us that the fullness of God is activated in a life of a believer who knows the love of God. This surpasses head knowledge. This is knowledge of the heart epignosis in the Greek, which means experiential knowledge. A knowing that comes through encounter. This is the importance of spending time in God's presence and God's word. You encounter Him in that place, and He tells you who you really are. You can't know a thing better that its manufacturer. All your life you've lived a life you were not created for, a life outside of God. Now Christ has brought you back to the Father's presence; you have access to His voice. In His presence, you are educated, you receive His love, He fills you with His fullness and because you no longer need love and acceptance from people, you preach the gospel to them. They may hate you or think you're a fool for it, but this has no relevance to the son who is surrendered. Legitimate sons of God choose to deny themselves, pick up their cross and follow Jesus. They live only to fulfil the will of God. I've been ignored, received evil stares, sworn at, mocked and ridiculed for my faith, but I will not stop because I'm living from the approval of my Heavenly Father. You've been affirmed as a son or a daughter, so you can't stop either.

Why did Peter and John say outright no to the Sanhedrin in the book of Acts when the Sanhedrin ordered them to stop preaching the gospel? (Acts 4) It was because they were living for the approval of one, their Heavenly Father.

They told the Sanhedrin, "Judge for yourselves whether it is right to obey man rather than God." What we fail to realise is that this is an issue of idolatry. We have esteemed the opinion of man over the truth of God. We have also esteemed our reputation before man over the Great Commission which beckons us to preach the gospel to all
creation. When they saw their courage, they knew they had been with Jesus, do you see the power of the presence of God for the works of sons?

The blessing of obedience when you are sent out from the presence

One morning I was in solitude and quietness with the lord, worshipping and adoring Him. I felt a leading from Him to ask on my social media platforms if people were in need of physical healing. I was obedient by His grace and on that day: a person with a back issue of about six years was healed, a man whose face was burnt on one side, woke up the next day with his skin significantly cleared up! Not all the people I prayed for that day were instantly healed; however I got the reward of my obedience which was showing the Father's heart and hand through my life and bringing joy and liberty to his children. There are a few things to learn from this encounter: 1) we can't cower in fear in the face of sicknesses and infirmities, rather we must adopts our Big Brother's perspective and see them as opportunities to reveal the Father's glory. 2) Giving my attention to God that morning allowed me to be more receptive to His instruction; the presence of God must be the foundation of the work of sons. 3) Prolonged pains and issues with the body may not be natural; they may be enforced by spirits of infirmities. Some bodily issues are work or stress related for instance those that come through fitness and exercise. In those cases ample time given to rest should relieve the pain. However when the pain is prolonged, we must ask whether the pain is being enforced by a spirit of infirmity which is a work of the devil that sons get to destroy.

Sons don't just go on outreach, they are an outreach

As we explored in the previous chapter, sons of

God are the embodiment of the presence of their Father. This means that sons are an opportunity for the heavenly Father to reach out and touch the world. Sons don't wait for outreach to reach out to people, they rather become an outreach.

It was a normal day, and I went for a haircut. I knew that it wasn't an official 'outreach'. As I was cutting my hair, I saw my barber holding his back and I heard him complaining about pains. I decided I was going to pray for him but to be completely honest, fear tried to hold me back. The reason for this is my older brother had told me about the arguments he and this barber of mine had about Jesus. So my thought process was he probably wouldn't let me pray because he is an antagonist of Christ who doesn't believe that the Lord is who He says He is. Anyway, I realised that I had nothing to lose. The worst that could happen was for him to say no. It can't be worse than that. If he kicked me out of the shop, then he would lose a customer and I would suffer persecution for the sake of Christ and be blessed for it! Anyway, I approached him and asked if I could pray for him; he consented. I laid hands on him and said a very simple prayer commanding his back to be healed; he was instantly healed; he couldn't believe it. The next time I went to the barbershop, I noticed the music that was playing was gospel. I don't know if he has completely turned to Christ, but I know God has started working on his heart.

This act of love and boldness opened up another door for evangelism and healings in my barber's shop. The other barber also had an issue with his back; one of his legs being shorter than the other affected it but God grew out his leg to even length with the other and completely healed his back. Now every time I go to cut my hair, God is the subject of the conversation, because my barbers share how I prayed for them and they received God's healing power. Many customers receive prayers because of this and I always have a platform to share Christ.

Revealing the Provider

This is not only about healings and miracles, although, I must admit, it's one of my favourites. There are many other avenues through which sons lay themselves down as opportunities for their Heavenly Father to flow through them and touch the world. The reality is this, when you know you are a son, you understand that your life is not yours but for the will of the Father. It is for the revelation of the character and nature of God. The truth is that radical generosity is a part of sons' responsibility to joyfully reveal the character and glory of the Father. I remember making a mistake and losing money because I ordered the wrong train ticket. The natural man can grumble and complain; however, sons of God are joyous in the flesh and their circumstances should be unable to steal their joy. In the presence of God, there is the fullness of joy and sons live in the presence of their Father; so the fruit must be joy. Joy is a fruit of the Spirit for a reason. I had to book a new train ticket which meant I was about to lose more money.

On my way back home with my friend, we saw a guy who was selling rap compact discs (CDs) and we decided to share the love of Christ with him. He was completely hostile to the message of the cross; he was angry at God because he felt God had neglected him. All of creation is waiting for the manifestation of the sons of God because it's through sons that they will see the true heart of the Father, as we see the Father through the Son of God, Jesus Christ. As he went on about why God wasn't real, God spoke to me and told me to bless him financially. A rival voice came straight after, as you can imagine, which reminded me that I had just lost a significant amount of money. Remember, I earlier stated that sons of God know that their lives are not their own but for the revelation of the nature of their Father. God is a giver, so why not show that through my life as a son of God. I marched to the cash machine, withdrew some money and gave it to him. His countenance changed; he became so much more receptive to the gospel. We preached and shared our testimony with him about how God saved us. After this, he decided to repent from his sins and turn to Christ as his Lord and Saviour. People need to hear the love of God; however, they also need to see it. That is where you come in. In fact, it's the reason you were created: to glorify your Heavenly Father.

The power of 'Jesus loves you'

I need you to understand the power and impact a statement as simple as Jesus loves you can have on a life and on eternity. I remember I was in my university library and I received a text from my partner. A soul had just repented from his sins and surrendered to Christ, and all she did was to tell him that Jesus loved him as she was waiting in the gym. After she told him Jesus loves him, he left his companions, went back to her and told her that he was born and raised an atheist, but he had always thought there is more to life. When she told him that Jesus loves him, he received the answer he needed. He went to church with her the following Sunday and responded to the altar call. This was such an encouragement to me. There are many times I have received cold shoulders from people I've reached out to by simply telling them that Jesus loves them, but when you have an encounter like that you know you can't stop. Every cold shoulder is worth it for that soul that responds to Christ.

Destroying condemnation, infirmities and creating hunger for the presence of God

Godly grief leads to repentance. However, worldly grief leads to condemnation. The wisdom of the world, as we learn in the third chapter of James is demonic. Therefore, demonic wisdom teaches people to grieve a kind of grief that leads to condemnation when they commit sins or even over their past sins. This, unfortunately, rules the heart of many Christians who let the lies of the enemy speak louder than the truth of God expressed through the cross of Christ - the truth of forgiveness and redemption.

Eddie was a victim of this work of the devil. He worked in Westfield, a shopping mall in Stratford, London England. My friend and I were near his stall and he asked us if we wanted to buy his nail product. My reply was, "No, we don't, but I would like to tell you that Jesus loves you and He has a great plan for your life." I also asked him if he had pain in his body. He then replied, "I love Jesus too, but I always do bad things that makes Jesus unhappy and it makes me feel really guilty." He added that he had had pain in his back for a while. This specific pain was a work of the devil because it was enforced by a spirit of infirmity. My friend and I encouraged him in the love of God that destroys condemnation, and we also asked if we could pray for him and for his back to be healed. He allowed us. I laid my hands on his back and began to pray. I also prayed against shame, condemnation and the sin that held him bound. I commanded that he would be free. As soon as I was done praying, I could see tears falling from his eyes; his back was completely healed. He said he felt something leave his back as we prayed. The entrance of God's Spirit is the eviction of another. He could tangibly feel the joyful presence of God that sons get to enforce in the lives of the people they encounter. God's kingdom had come to this man.

After this happened, God spoke to my heart and asked if I really wanted to show this man His love. He said if I do, I should buy his product from him. I decided to be obedient; I bought the product which I had no use for. He was overwhelmed with joy and told us that this was his first day on the job and no one had purchased an item all day. I was his first customer! Then he then said something that will stay with me for the rest of my life. He said, "I want to come with you where you are going, because I know you are going to meet with God and I want to be there as well." We encouraged him with the truth of the access he has to the presence of God through Jesus Christ. Sin, infirmities and condemnation (works of the devil) get destroyed in the life of a man through sons who carry the presence of their Father. This is a reality accessible to every son of God.

A hope and a future restored

There was a boy with hopes and dreams of becoming a footballer in the future. Football was his passion and throughout his years in school, he stood out as a talented and gifted footballer. However a medical condition stood in the way of his dreams and ambition from becoming a reality. He was plagued with a bone disease; there was a chipped bone in his hip. The doctor suggested surgery and implanting a prosthetic bone in the area that was chipped, but they could not guarantee that it would be successful. This boy worked hard to keep his dream alive physically but gave up in his heart. This condition meant he could not play to the level he knew he could in his heart.

I met this young man at a youth retreat. He narrated his dreams and how his medical condition has been a Goliath in his life in pursuing his dream. Believing my Father is a healer and the God who has plans of good and not of evil for His children, and a Father who gives His children a hope and a future, I laid my hand on his hips and began to command a creative work to occur in there. To my amazement, a bone snapped into place in his hip! Every bit of pain, clicking and grinding was eradicated. This young man cried for a while after the healing occurred! Not only because he was healed but because the Father restored in him the hope of being a footballer in the future. If sin never came into the world, then sicknesses and diseases would have never come into it. Sickness is the fruit of sin, which came from the devil that tempted and influenced Adam and Eve to fall. The devil has worked to bring about illnesses and diseases that have taken the hopes and dreams of many away from them. How many

Matthews do we have in our families, see in shopping malls and walk past every day. Many are waiting for an encounter with the Heavenly Father that will come through His sons and daughters. The Father gets to restore their hope and future through our obedience.

Encountering heaven through sons of God

Sons are ambassadors of God's kingdom and the embodiment of His presence as I previously mentioned. Because of this, people get to encounter heaven when they encounter God's sons. Heaven is the perfect illustration of the kingdom of God because it is the realm that completely bows to His dominion and consequently, it is the realm that enjoys the greatest measure of God's presence. Heaven is active in the spirit of a surrendered son who has availed himself to be an ambassador of God. The beauty is that this doesn't only have to be a theory or concept but a reality in the life of sons of God. People have the opportunity to encounter the kingdom and presence of God that they carry.

It was a Sunday and a young man walked into church with crutches. Rather than seeing a problem, I saw a perfect opportunity for earth to conform to heaven through this specific situation. I saw an opportunity to show what the resurrection of Jesus made available to this young, church-going Christian who was yet to completely surrender to God. I laid my hands on his knee and began to pray. I prayed three times. After the first time, he said he felt a sense of relief and he could walk slightly better than he could earlier on. The second time, he said it felt like air was entering his knee; it's interesting how the Holy Spirit came like a rushing wind when the disciples encountered Him in the Upper Room (Acts 2). The third time, he said, "It feels heavenly." He could feel the atmosphere of heaven in his knee. I must admit there was a HUGE sense of God's presence around me even as I prayed. So, I know exactly what he was talking about. Guess what? His crutches were rendered useless that day. He told me that he got injured because a kid from school decided to trip him up. That thought had to come from somewhere and it resulted in an injury that warranted crutches. The devil is sly and cunning. I'm sure the kid who tripped him up did not premeditate injuring him and putting him on crutches. Nevertheless, the work of the devil was destroyed and little Tobi got a taste of heaven. God's kingdom is at work.

Accidental healings and miracles happen when sons carry the presence of the Father!

In the book of Acts we see that people were being healed by Peter's shadow, (Acts 5:15) we also read of when people touched Jesus Christ and were instantly healed. An example, is the woman with the issue of blood (Matthew 9:20). Well, this occurred because of the presence of the Father that they carried. Psalm 91:1 says this, "He who dwells in the secret place of the Most High Shall abide under the shadow of the Almighty" (Psalms☐91:1☐ NKJV☐☐). Bill Johnson said this: "You will always release the shadow of whatever overshadows you."
Peter dwelt in the secret place with God; he spent much time in God's presence, as did Jesus. Because of this, they carried the presence of God and 'accidental miracles' occurred. Peter was overshadowed by the presence of God in the secret place and the presence that overshadowed him healed people without his knowledge or consent. When you put a sponge in a sink full of water for a while, and you take the sponge out, the substance of the water remains on the sponge. God's presence is the water, you are the sponge.

We make a mistake when we look at accounts like this in scripture and say that's Jesus or that's Peter. We must understand that the same Spirit in them is the same in us. We don't have a junior Holy Spirit. What we must ask is what their process was? As I mentioned before, we find the key in psalm 91: they learnt how to abide in the secret place. They learnt to abide in the presence of God.

I remember going to a campus fellowship in Hull to preach. It was a fantastic time in God's presence! I stayed at a friend of mine's house who studied in Hull. He was visited by a friend of his. As soon as I saw her, God spoke to me about her back, and her uneven legs. I checked it and I saw that they were not equal, I looked away and I looked back and they were completely equal, this shocked me! No prayer had been uttered, she checked her back and it was completely healed! She bent down and touched her toes and prior to this encounter, she could not touch them! What blew my mind even more was that she had a really bad shin pain which I had no knowledge about, and we said no prayer for, but it just seemed to vanish. She looked for it but couldn't find! She was overwhelmed and I was astonished!

I recall three other occasions were short legs which caused people really bad back pains seemed to be growing out on their own accord, I should say on the accord of the Holy Spirit. One was when I was evangelising in Croydon England and I encountered a homeless person on the street. The second was in my third year of university at Abide Fellowship (the campus ministry I oversee) and the third is really dear to my heart because it was in the comfort of my house. The recipient of the creative miracle was my elder brother.

I recall another time when I visited my friend, Famous, in Manchester. He has ambitious parents! "Haha"! We saw a homeless man on the street and God gave me a word of knowledge about his knee and I prayed for him. After laying hands and praying, he testified to feeling heat on his knee and the pain was completely healed! The fire of the Holy Spirit burnt away the pain. I was also shocked and amazed to find out that the back pain I never prayed about, or had knowledge about was also completely healed! When God moves this way, it humbles you; you realise the works of healings and miracles are done by God's presence and His presence alone.

The Deliverer revealed and purpose birthed

God delivered the children of Israel from what had bound them for over 400 years in Egypt. The same God who delivered them is the same God who is delivering people now. Jesus Christ is the same yesterday, today and forever. Sons operate in the authority of their Father and God's authority over sin and addictions is revealed in the resurrection of Jesus Christ. Being a witness of the resurrection of Jesus Christ is not just a matter of telling people that Christ rose from the dead but demonstrating the power of His resurrection. The disciples would not have had to wait in Jerusalem for the promise of the Father which was the presence of the Holy Spirit and power, if being witnesses was just about speaking of the resurrection. Jesus said after they were endued with power from on high that they would be witnesses. The disciples were to be witnesses of what? They were to be witnesses of His resurrection.

Sons have the privilege of being able to witness

Jesus' resurrection by enforcing what the resurrection makes possible in the lives of those that encounter them. Jesus' resurrection from the dead means that He has all authority and power over: death, sin, sickness and addictions.

During the first year Abide Fellowship, a girl named Blessing asked me in one of the meetings to pray for her against the spirit of fear. She spoke to me about how God has blessed her with a voice to sing and worship. However, she couldn't because she was crippled by fear. Whenever it came to singing in front of people, terror would consume her, and she would not be able to do it. I knew this was a demonic influence and so I prayed for her. The next time I saw her, she was on the stage as a member of a choir for a gospel production named Transcend. When I spoke to her about it, she said the fear was completely gone. She testified that she felt an electrical current go through her body as I prayed. That current was a manifestation of the presence of God which produces liberty for those in bondage and releases them into purpose!

I remember praying after my second year as an undergraduate, asking God to give me opportunities to impact students on my course with the power of the gospel, for His glory. In my third year, a girl on my course was led to Christ and her addiction to marijuana was broken. God is powerful and He longs to reveal His power and love through His sons and daughters!

Arthritis, broken cartilage and torn ligament healed

One of the things I love about being a conduit for the manifestation of the love and power of God is the freedom and joy that it brings to people! I love showing people God's love for them and I love seeing it overwhelm them. A woman from my church battled with years of arthritis which deeply affected her knee. She told me she couldn't walk without feeling agonising pain. She told me she would always miss her bus because she couldn't walk fast enough to catch it. After praying for her, God healed her! She got on her knees and began to crawl without pain and she thanked God. She worshipped Him, and it was such a sight!

I recall evangelising in Stratford England, and I came across a homeless man with a broken cartilage in his knee. After a short prayer he was completely healed. He began to kick the bin to test it and he felt no pain. He told me that I am a powerful man, but I understand that the power is really God's presence. I have learnt to carry and steward God's presence to a measure and I'm pressing in for more! You should too! If I was a powerful man, then you have every reason to read as a spectator. However, if God's presence is what is powerful, and you know you have access to the Father through the cross, then your response should be a conviction to press into God's presence. Not because you want to heal or possess power for the sake of it, but because you effectively want to witness Christ's resurrection, reveal the glory of the Father on the earth, destroy the works of the devil and bring Joy and liberty to people.

I remember seeing on twitter, a tweet from a person I know. He tweeted about an injury that rendered him to the sidelines. He is a footballer. He tweeted that 'the doctor said he can't play football for five weeks, but he is going to believe in God's report'. I loved his faith and I reached out to him to pray for him, he consented, and so I called him. After a short prayer his sprained ankle and the torn ligament in his foot was completely healed.

Don't be misinformed!

I don't want you to be misinformed by the number of testimonies you've read in this chapter. There are countless occasions when people were hostile to the message of the cross. A seed was planted nonetheless. I also don't want you to get discouraged when you pray for the sick and nothing happens. I don't let it discourage me. I press into the presence of God and continue to take risks in the open. I also do not want you to think you can't preach the gospel because you don't see healings occur through your life. If you don't and you desire the spiritual gift, ask for it in faith. Paul says we should earnestly desire the spiritual gifts with love being the foundation and motive (1 Cor. 14:1). Your motive is the revelation of the Father and God is love; you need the gift of healing to show people that your Father is a healer. This is why healing and miracles are by-products of sonship. What I hope this chapter has done is create hunger in your spirit to seek God's presence and to be empowered by His presence to preach the gospel of the kingdom of God as well as demonstrate it in power. The kingdom of God is not in talk but in power, as Paul says.

Gifts like giving, service, prophecy and miracles do not define the son; the Father defines the son. The gifts just serve as simple tools for the revelation of the Father and they equip sons to be expressions of outreach in diverse ways. They help us minister and work the works of sons. We fall into error if we find ourselves through the fact that people are healed and delivered, through the fact that we are prophesying, or giving. These things are the by-products of sonship; they are the doings of the Spirit whilst we are simply His channels.

Represent the Father; people's eternity depends on it

In the High Priest's prayer in the seventeenth chapter of John's Gospel, Jesus said this: "And this is eternal life, that they know you, the only true God, and Jesus Christ whom you have sent" (John 17:3 ESV). It simply means that eternal life is knowing the Father and the Son. A knowing that speaks of intimacy. This reveals the importance of sons. The reason sons exist is to reveal their Father and make Him known, so that those who don't know Him are presented with the opportunity of having eternal life. Jesus said this in the same chapter, "I glorified you on earth, having accomplished the work that you gave me to do" (John 17:4 ESV).

We understand through this passage of scripture the part sons of God have to play in people coming to eternal life. When we live lives that glorify God as Christ did, we will make Him known to the world around us. This in turn gives unbelievers an opportunity to know exactly what the Father is like. If many people saw the Father for who He really is, they would forsake their sins and turn to Him to be their Father. Thus, all of creation is waiting for the manifestation of the sons of God.

Apostle John this: 'as many as received Him, to them he gave the right to be sons of God (John1:12); we receive Christ by faith. Jesus said that those who believe in Him will do the same things that He did and even greater things for He goes to the Father John (14:12). Through faith in Christ: we become sons of God and we are empowered to work the works of son, which is ultimately to reveal the Father.

Intimacy with God is the key as the scriptures says: '...the people that do know their God shall be strong and shall do exploits' (Daniel 11:32. The root meaning of exploits is heroic deeds. Furthermore the knowledge spoken of here is experiential knowledge. Heroes save and deliver those oppressed. Therefore through faith: we receive Christ, become sons, know God experientially, do His works, reveal the Father and destroy the works of the devil.

Chapter 7: The Chastising of Sons (Suffering into Glory)

- 'Correction is only seen as judgement to those who still love their sin.'
- 'Discipline is choosing between what you want now and what you want most'
- 'When we suffer for Christ's sake we should do so not only with courage but

with joy.'

Chapter 7: The Chastising of Sons (Suffering into Glory)

Discipline is evidence that you're truly a son

Naturally, a father disciplines his son and his son matures as a result of that discipline, teaching and training of his father. What we have in the context where a father fails to discipline his children are the sons of Eli, Hophni and Phinehas, who rebelled against God and cost their family line relinquishing the position of service to God as priests. Lack of discipline killed them, literally. We learnt from the author of Proverbs that one of the most significant forms of deliverance, especially for children is discipline. The word of God says, "Do not withhold discipline from a child; if you strike him with a rod, he will not die" (Proverbs 23:13 ESV).

It means that discipline has the power to deliver a child from death. Discipline is one of the most effective forms of deliverance. The author of Proverbs also says that folly is bound up in the heart of a child, but the rod of discipline drives it far from him (Proverbs 22:15). We can compare foolishness to a spirit that discipline delivers a child from.

The author of Hebrew encouraged believers with this truth, "And have you forgotten the exhortation that addresses you as sons? My son, do not regard lightly the discipline of the Lord, nor be weary when reproved by Him. For the Lord disciplines the one He loves, and chastises every son whom He receives" (Hebrews 12:5-6 ESV). The very fact that we are reproved and chastised by our Heavenly Father is proof that we are His children and He disciplines us in order to mature us. Without discipline, a child remains a child but with discipline, a child becomes a son. Of Jesus, Prophet Isaiah wrote, "Unto us a child is born and unto us a Son is given" (Isaiah 9:6).

When you are born again, you become a child of God, but you can only be given to impact the world, when you've matured to son's status. Christians who have significant impact on the world are not the ones with the title of prophet, evangelist, apostle, teacher or pastor, but the ones who have been trained and disciplined by their Heavenly Father and through His discipline have become sons of God. A son without a title will always have more impact that one who has a title but is not a son. Sonship will always be greater than servanthood. Romans 8:14 is a verse we all love to quote: "Those who are led by the Spirit are called the sons of God." This is a great verse. However, the word sons used here is the Greek word huios, which refers to a fully-mature son. So, if we quote this verse again with its true meaning in mind, it will sound like this, "Those who are led by the Spirit are called the matured sons of God." □□□□□□□□□□□□□□□□□□□□□□□□□□□ □□□□

What is significant about a huios (a fully mature son) is that this son consistently resembles the Father in word and deed. The key is in the fact that he is led by the Spirit. God is Spirit and His kingdom is also in the Spirit. If they are led by the Spirit, it means they are not driven by what they see - what is earthly and carnal. They live by faith, which is the evidence of things hoped for and the conviction of things not seen. As a result of being spiritual, they are able to represent God and His kingdom very well and consistently because there is nothing carnal about God and His world. Mature sons are heavenly in nature, impacting and changing the earth with the culture of heaven.

The truth is that it takes serious discipline and maturity to be led by the Spirit and not your flesh and emotion. The culture of this world is very sensual; it is feelings-orientated and this world teaches people to be driven by what they see. It takes studying in the classroom of God to be spiritually led. It takes: growing in the word of righteousness, studying the word of God, denying yourself, picking up your cross and following Christ. It takes suffering. As a son who wants to represent God well you must understand that you have to suffer into glory.

Suffering into glory

Living by faith is suffering because we haven't been trained to live that way. It's not something that comes naturally. It takes staying very close to Jesus, the author and finisher of our faith and becoming a product of His example rather than our circumstances. Paul says in Galatians 4 that we are no longer slaves to the elements of the world. We are no longer products of our circumstances. We have now overcome and outgrown the things we experienced whilst we were orphans and immature. God is our Potter and has remoulded us and our response.

Growing up as a teenager in secondary school, if someone said, "Your mum" to me as a means to be verbally abusive, I would respond, with: "Your mum" as well. Then if he called me another name, I would respond with another name. Can you see how I've become a product of my circumstance? What is happening to me is that in responding in the way I am, I'm becoming a product of my circumstance. The person speaking is the potter and I'm the clay, because he is shaping and directing my response. Many make people who offend them their god, because they mould them to be bitter in response. Thus, they become products of their circumstance.

However, what we see in Christ is holiness that takes maturity, and we have the key of how Jesus was able to reveal the Father. He suffered by not being a product of His circumstance. He did not call down angels to avenge Him when soldiers came to arrest Him even though He could have; doing that would have made Him a slave to His circumstances. He did not drop the cross when the ones He came to die for beat Him, spat at Him and mocked Him. That would have made Him clay and His circumstance His potter. When faced with fear and anxiety in the garden of Gethsemane, when the reality of everything He was going to go through on the cross was standing right before Him, living by His circumstances would have led Him to disregard the will of God and run away from the cross.

Now what does the fear and anxiety from the garden, the arrest in the garden and the mockery, beating and spit from the soldiers have in common? They are all different forms of sufferings. It makes sense then that the author of Hebrews said this, "For it was fitting that He, for whom and by whom all things exist, in bringing many sons to glory, should make the founder of their salvation perfect through suffering" (Hebrews 2:10 ESV). In Luke's gospel, Jesus responded like this after it was reported to Him that Herod was seeking His life, "And He said to them, "Go, tell that fox, 'Behold, I cast out demons and perform cures today and tomorrow, and the third day I shall be perfected" (Luke 13:32 NKJV). It wasn't healing or deliverance that made Jesus perfect, it was His death and suffering, it was the trials He faced, because trials and tribulations produce perfection. It is important to note that the words "perfection" and "complete" are synonymous to maturity. The Greek word is "teleios", which means to mature from going through necessary stages to reach a completed goal. In the case of Christ's suffering, it was the necessary process He needed to go through to be perfected. The process matured Him and ensured that He completed His goal. This is why James 1:2-4; Hebrews 12:2; Romans 8:18 and Luke 24:26 are such key verses for us as believers.

James 1:2-4 (NKJV)

"My brethren, count it all joy when you fall into various trials, knowing that the testing of your faith produces patience. Knowing that the testing of your faith produces patience. But let patience have its perfect work, that you may be perfect and complete, lacking nothing."

Hebrews 12:2 (NKJV)

"Looking unto Jesus, the author and finisher of our faith, who for the joy that was set before Him endured the cross, despising the shame, and has sat down at the right hand of the throne of God."

Romans 8:18 (NKJV)

"For I consider that the sufferings of this present time are not worthy to be compared with the glory which shall be revealed in us."

Luke 24:26 NKJV

"Ought not the Christ to have suffered these things and to enter into His glory?"

These different verses drive home the same point: the process that matures us and brings us into perfection or completion is trial (suffering). When we are fully mature, then revealing the glory of God becomes second nature; thus we suffer into glory.

The result of this is that, like Christ, we are no longer products of our circumstances, living by the events of this world, but sons of God living by faith. We live by the example of Christ. Rather than slapping back when we are slapped, we turned the other cheek because 'sin against us cannot produce sin in us' as Dan Mohler says. It means that fear loses its dominion over us. We may feel it, but if it stops us from fulfilling the will of God, we will be falling short of our Father's expectation. It would be hard to tell if we are truly maturing, without the tests and that is why they are needed. How do you respond when people wrong you? Do you harbour offense or do you overcome evil with good? How do you feel when you experience fear whenever you are about to evangelise? Do you let it cripple you, or do you act in the obedience to the word of God anyway? When temptation comes and there is the urge to indulge in sin, are you going to be a product of your feeling or the product of the word of God, which calls you to be holy as He is holy?"

These circumstances are to test you; they are to try you and through them you mature and come to perfection. Consequently, you will be able to manifest the Father well because they see to it that you grow in the fruit of the Spirit: love, joy, peace, patience, kindness, gentleness, faithfulness and self-control

Love for God and His glory is what compels the endurance of sons

The reason for the discipline is that you will be a partakers of God's holiness as the writer of Hebrews said (Hebrews 12:10). It's your love for God that will enable you to endure the suffering that comes through His chastising.
If you love God, you would want His name to be glorified. Therefore, you will endure the discomfort of trials and tribulations because you believe that God's glory is worth it.

Jesus endured the cross because of His love for the Father. We must understand that it was Jesus's total love expressed through His submission to God that compelled Him to go to the cross.

The strength to love and suffer by laying down His life for you and me came through His submission to the will of His Father. This is true because in the garden, after He asked the cup of suffering to pass Him by, He said, "Not as I will but as you will." If it was down to His will, He probably would not have gone to the cross. But the strength to love you and me and lay down His life came from His submission to the Father, which is empowered by love. Again, Jesus said in John 14:15 that if we love Him we will obey His commandments. Submission is made possible by love. So, we see that the strength to submit to the process of suffering into the glory of God like Christ comes through submission to the will and process the Father lays for us; what gives us the strength to submit to God is our love and devotion to Him.

Jesus said in the Gospel of John, "Unless a kernel of wheat falls into the ground and dies, it remains alone but when it dies, it bears much fruit." When Jesus came into world, He stood alone as the begotten Son of God; the word begotten means kind. Meaning Jesus stood alone as the Son of God's kind, all others were orphans fathered by the lies of the enemy.

Remember sons are living manifestations of the glory of God. So the sheer love of God and His glory in Christ compelled Him to die and produce more sons so that He no longer stands alone as a Son of God's kind. Again, the reason for Jesus' love is the glory of the Father. He died so that more sons would be produced who will be able to glorify the Father. He suffered for the sake of the glory of God.

If we want the end of Jesus which is glory, then we must welcome His process as well which is suffering, Paul puts it like this in the third chapter in His epistle to the church at Philippi, "That I may know Him and the power of His resurrection, and the fellowship of His sufferings, being conformed to His death..." (Philippians□ 3:10□ NKJV□□). He understood that you can't have the former without the latter and the latter is the route to the former. The fellowship of His suffering and conforming to His death is the route to knowing the power of His resurrection. In order to resurrect, you first have to die. Before the glory of childbirth, there is the suffering of labour. □□□□□□□□□□□□□

Abraham knew what it meant to join in the fellowship of God's suffering; he knows the pain of actually deciding to sacrifice his son. Obviously he didn't do it in the end because God stopped him; however deciding to do it would have still been painful. Hosea also can relate to God's suffering on an intimate level, because he knows what it feels like to join to an unfaithful bride, who he had to remain committed and merciful to. God will sometimes allow our suffering, not because He hates us, but because He wants us to know Him more intimately. Our suffering has everything to do with enjoying deeper intimacy with God and being able to communicate God's life more clearly to the world. You simply cannot be one with God and you cannot reveal the glory of God without suffering. Jesus came to His own and His own rejected Him. Jesus shows that God's glory is not just shown in power (healing and miracles), it's also shown in suffering for the sake of love. The

Pharisees (religious system) and the Romans (world system) killed Him in their rebellion and disobedience. Jesus' death and suffering communicated how Adam (humanity) rejected and killed the life of the Father in him and on the earth. It can't be overemphasised that we literally learn everything we need to know about the Father when we look at Jesus, even His death and resurrection. When Jesus forgave those who put Him on the cross, it tells the tale of how God never gave up on mankind and continues to forgive us who killed His life in us with our sin. The reality is that we continue to kill God's life in us, every time we sin. Hebrew 6:6 makes it clear that we crucify the saviour yet again. But Jesus' blood cries mercy; He beckons sinners to come to Him for forgiveness, revealing the heart of the Father and His desire for His lost sheep to return to Him.

Whatever way or form you currently know Christ through the fellowship of His suffering, find solace in this: you look so much like Jesus. You are fulfilling your created purpose. You are manifesting His life so clearly and you are enjoying a deep level of intimacy with your

Heavenly Father. You know His hurt and you can relate to His pain. Oh what an honour and privilege we get to share in the suffering of our God! And we do it to His glory!

How to deal with trials and suffering as sons

Perspective is everything. You deal with seasons of trials and suffering by seeing them as what they are, seasons of maturity. Seasons that is preparing you for greater glory. Our elder brother, Jesus Christ, understood this. Whenever Jesus Christ wanted to talk about His death, He would say, "Now it's time for the son of man to be glorified" (John 12:23). He focused on the end. Focusing on the end will make it easier for you to go through the means. In pregnancy the joy of childbirth enables the woman to go through the suffering of labour. You may be in a season of trials and tribulations right now, find solace in the fact that if you submit to the discipline and chastising of your Father who loves you, you are on your way to being a clearer revelation of Him because you're growing to a greater degree of maturity.

"Now no chastening seems to be joyful for the present, but painful; nevertheless, afterward it yields the peaceable fruit of righteousness to those who have been trained by it" (Hebrews 12:11 NKJV). Let's focus on what the suffering, that's coming through the chastising of the Lord, will produce whilst we go through the process. □□□□□□□□□□□□□

My process and glory

What I've written in this chapter are the things the Holy Spirit taught me through the Holy Scriptures at the beginning of 2017. It was as if He was preparing me for what I was going to face during the year. God is beautiful in that He will speak to you directly and He will also speak to you through His body. I remember receiving a call from a prophet friend of mine from America who told me that God had shown him a dream concerning me. In this dream, he saw me as a man with no arms and legs. He said I reminded him of this particular evangelist named Nick Vujicic. He said in the dream, there was an open door afar off and I was trying to get to the door. However, there were major obstacles in my way. He said with much striving through tests and obstacles, I got to the door and behind the door there were many ministry opportunities for me.

What the prophet and I didn't know at the time is that at the end of the year I would be ordained as an Evangelist, and there would be various opportunities for ministry. However, before the honour and glory of being confirmed and used as an expression of the ministry and glory of Jesus on earth, my relationship with my beloved was majorly tested. I considered what life would be like if I backslid because of the magnitude of testing and temptations I was facing. The fear of pursuing God's call made my past seem a bit more appealing (I was in the garden of Gethsemane). I felt dry, even after preaching and seeing people healed. At times; I felt like God took away measures of His grace from me, and just left me to fight on my own. I would find myself crying to God, asking Him what was going on. His still small voice would remind me that I must suffer into glory. Besides, the Holy Spirit would remind me that Jesus was interceding for me.

I soon realised that I would be ordained as an evangelist at the end of the year. Then it all made sense. God prepared me by telling me that the process to glory is trial. Because of the glory

I would come into at the end of the year, the enemy never wanted me to get there. So, he tempted me to forsake God's call and return to my past. God used this to try me and bring me to maturity. What the enemy meant for evil, God meant it for good. The enemy attacked me in so many ways but the one thing I would not allow him to attack was the secret place. If the enemy can take away your access into the secret place with God, then he can take away your spiritual life. The secret place was where God refined my perspective, encouraged me, picked me up and strengthened me. God enabled me to feel His jealousy over me and led me to consecrate myself to prayer and fasting as Jesus did before His ministry began in the wilderness. God said to me, "For most of this year (2017) you've been in the wilderness like the children of Israel. Now, you are about to step into Jesus' wilderness." In this wilderness, God met me with His voice and presence, and I encountered Him in ways I had never before. He opened up a realm in the spirit to me, named the bridal realm (that's another book entirely). He spoke to me regarding identity, purpose and destiny and He filled me with grace. I consecrated into my ordination as

God's evangelist.

Here's the lesson. The enemy may be throwing bombs at you to derail and destroy you because he is after your calling, identity and purpose. You can either let his attacks push you away from the Father's arms and embrace or you can let it push you to God. You must understand that trials and testing are what God uses to refine your character. In order for God to refine you, you need to come to Him. His presence and voice will wash and clean you up. His presence and voice will prune you. The enemy is a pawn in the game. If you have the right perspective, you will allow the temptations and tests he throws at you to push you to God so that He may clean, prune and refine you. God does this because glory is destructive to the immature. Maturity is built in God's presence, and it makes you ready to carry God's glory (weight). God's glory is the revelation of who He is and it is the mature that also reveal Him.

Choose this day to submit to the process and suffer into glory.

2 Corinthians 4:17-18

"For our light affliction, which is but for a moment, is working for us a far more exceeding and eternal weight of
glory, 18 while we do not look at the things which are seen, but at the things which are not seen. For the things which are
seen are temporary, but the things which are not seen are eternal."

Chapter 8: A Son's Prayer

'The prayers of God's sons are effectual, fervent and avail much. Because they come from righteous hearts, they move mountains and change things to the glory of God. When God's sons pray, great things happen.

Chapter 8: A Son's Prayer

The Bible encourages us to come boldly to the throne of grace to receive mercy and find grace to help in the time of need (Hebrews 4:16). The Psalmist praised God for giving him his heart's desire and for not withholding the requests of His lips (Psalm 21:2). Similarly, Isaiah prophesied that before we call God will answer and while we are still speaking He will hear (Isaiah 65:24). These privileges are for sons (heirs and heiresses) of God and His kingdom. Jesus further revealed the unquantifiable grace that sons enjoy from the Father when they pray to Him. At the tomb of Lazarus, He lifted His eyes to heaven and said, "Father, I thank You that You have heard Me. And I know that You always hear Me..."(John 11:41-42). Beloved, as long as you are a son, the

Father is ready and willing to answer your prayer so that you can bring glory to Him every day of your life.

Here are son's prayer and Bible-based confessions you should say regularly:

I am God's beloved son, a family member of the Godhead, seated in His love and acceptance, in Him I live and move and bear His image. I am God's reflection, the brightness of His glory, the express image of His person, a legacy of His love. He has crowned me with His grace and arrayed me in His glory. His face shines upon me and He has made me His friend.

The Spirit of the Lord is upon me. His hands shall heal and serve through mine. His outstretched arm shall find the lost through my own. His Word shall be made flesh through my life.
I am neither too weak nor too small

to fulfil my call. I am neither too sinful nor flawed to be refused His grace. I am His chosen son. I am accepted, not because of my works but because of the finished works done on the cross by the Lord Jesus Christ.

The Father and I are one. He has given me His signet ring. I am anointed for such a time as this. I am called to produce much fruit. I have been raised up to take territory. I am ordained to bring heaven to earth. I am chosen to conquer. I am His double-edged sword. I am His Holy battle axe held in His hand, died and raised again to live a life of love.

I bear the fruits of the Father through both love and power. Kindness and humility are on my tongue, boldness and authority gird my loins. Performing miracles are in my nature and compassion and surrender are my closest companions. I am called to diffuse His fragrance of peace and show forth His manifold power.

The Lord has given me an invitation to His love and called me to feast upon Him. I am called to be near Him. As deep calls unto deep, daily I shall go into a deeper place of His love. His Grace and mercy cling to me. He will never grow weary of me. He will never turn His face from mine. He will never forsake me. He shall never be ashamed of me. He lavishly offers me forgiveness; He declares that I shall know His kindness. I am His son when I'm shining; I am His son even when suffering. I am crowned with my inheritance as an heir.

There is no condemnation against me because I am in Christ Jesus. I walk not after the flesh, but after the Spirit. For the law of the Spirit of life in Christ Jesus has set me free from the law of sin and death. Sin will not have dominion over me. The Almighty God will keep me from falling and present me blameless before His throne. It is written that being justified by faith, I have peace with God through Jesus Christ our Lord. Through the finished work of Jesus on the cross of Calvary, I have resounding victory over the devil, sin and the world. Thanks be unto God who has given me the victory through Jesus Christ my Saviour and Lord and blessed be God who causes me to triumph always in Christ. I am more than a conqueror through Christ Jesus who loved me and gave Himself for me.

My life is hid with Christ and Christ in God. I am covered by the precious, shielding and sheltering blood of Jesus. No weapon formed against me shall prosper. God will bless the work of my hands and the fruit of my body. I will not labour in vain nor bring forth for trouble. My spirit, soul and body as well as all that concern me shall continuously prosper, in Jesus' mighty name.

By faith, I receive the sevenfold anointing of the Messiah: the spirit of Lord is resting upon me, the spirit of wisdom and understanding, the spirit of counsel and might, the spirit of knowledge and of the fear of the LORD.

I declare with faith in my heart that I have the spirit of wisdom and revelation in the knowledge of God. The eyes of my understanding are enlightened and by the help of the Holy Spirit, I know the hope of God's calling and the riches of the glory of His inheritance in the saints as well as the exceeding greatness of His power towards us who believe, according to the working of His mighty power which He wrought in Christ, when He raised him from the dead, and set him at His own right hand in the heavenly places, far above principalities and power and might, and dominion, and every name that is named, not only in this world, but also in that which is to come.

I am the salt of the earth and the light of the world, a city built on a hill that cannot be hidden. My light will always shine brightly; men will see my good works and glorify my father who is in heaven.

I am a citizen of Zion, God's foremost ambassador. I am washed in the blood of the Lamb, clothed in God's righteousness and standing in His favour. I am seated with Christ Jesus in the heavenly places far above principalities and power. I declare that the fullness of the Godhead bodily dwells in Jesus and I am complete in him who is the head of all principalities and power. I have been ordained and anointed to enforce God's dominion and dispense His grace in my generation. I am an heir of the kingdom and a kingdom builder. I enjoy the indwelling, abiding and empowering presence of God, therefore I cannot fail. I am for signs and wonders. As God's son and heir of His kingdom, all things are mine. Nothing will hinder me, rob me or short-change me from enjoying my rights, privileges, inheritance and blessings as God's son, in Jesus' mighty name

Chapter 9: Wisdom Nuggets from the Author

'My son, give attention to my words; Incline your ear to my sayings. Do not let them depart from your eyes; Keep them in the midst of your heart; For they *are* life to those who find them, And health to all their flesh.' Proverbs 4:20-22(NKJV)

Chapter 9: Wisdom Nuggets from the Author

The book, "God's Son, God's Glory" is filled with wisdom nuggets from the first to the last chapter. Here are some of the timeless truths for your meditation and positive action steps:

✓ If the nature of God is not being revealed through your life, then there is no meaning to the breath you inhale and exhale. Who we are and what we are created for totally hang on this truth.

✓ God's perfect will is to see many of His sons on earth revealing His nature and, in doing so, extending His kingdom on earth as it is in heaven.

✓ Being rooted in your identity, intimate and submitted to God is the greatest tool for fulfilling your divine purpose on earth.

✓ Christ came to restore what Adam lost.

✓ Adam represents humanity. When Adam sinned, humanity sinned and fell short of the glory of God. That is, humanity fell from fulfilling its reason for being: to glorify God and reveal His nature through human life.

✓ You become a walking dead when you are not living the life and fulfilling the purpose you were created for.

✓ Three keys are needed for man to fulfil his divine purpose on earth: identity, submission and intimacy.

✓ Every kind of sin known to man has a common agenda: to attack our worship to God which encompasses our submission and obedience to His will. Think of a sin you can commit without relinquishing your submission to God.

✓ When the enemy is tempting you, he is presenting to you the option of worshipping and obeying something other than God, and that thing is the devil. When you succumb to the temptation, for a moment, you switch masters, and in doing so, you switch the context for your life and the person who defines you. Essentially, you switch your God.

✓ Slavery is the result when you are not in the presence of God. You become a slave to sin, a slave to the enemy, a slave to yourself, a slave to the opinions of man and society. Freedom can only be found in the presence of God.

✓ If your relationship with God is your biggest pursuit, not even sin can stop you from pursuing it. Spend time in Abba's presence and watch liberty come to you. It's a promise, "Wherever the Spirit of the Lord is, there is liberty."

✓ As we spend time in His presence, the Holy Spirit who is the power of God conforms us to the image of Christ so that His person can be displayed through our lives. The presence of God empowers us to be what we've been created to be - sons of God.

✓ One of the fruits of our sonship is that the works of the devil is being destroyed through our lives. One of the ways in which sons destroy the works of the devil is through evangelism.

✓ Whether you're an evangelist or not, if you

love God and people, (the two greatest commandments), you will evangelise and destroy the works of the devil.

✓ As human beings, who want to be accepted and loved by people and who don't want to come across as foolish, who care so much about reputation, preaching the gospel to unbelievers is tasking. But when we understand that we are sons of God, loved by a perfect Father, accepted in the beloved, then we will willingly become foolish to the world because what our Heavenly Father thinks of us matters more.

✓ The fullness of God is activated in a life of a believer who knows the love of God. This surpasses head knowledge. It is epignosis, knowledge of the heart. A knowing that comes through encounter. This is the importance of spending time in God's presence and God's word.

✓ Heaven is active in the spirit of a surrendered son who has availed himself to be an ambassador of God. The beauty is that this doesn't only have to be a theory or concept but a reality in the life of sons God. People have the opportunity to encounter the kingdom and presence of God that they carry.

✓ You may be in a season of trials and tribulations right now, find solace in the fact that if you submit to the discipline and chastising of your Father who loves you, you are on your way to being a clearer revelation of who He is because you're growing to a greater degree of maturity.

✓ The enemy may be throwing bombs at you to derail and destroy you because he is after your calling, identity and purpose. You can either let his attacks push you away from the Father's arms and embrace or you can let it push you to God.

✓ the enemy is a pawn in the game. If you have the right perspective, you will allow the tests he throws at you to push you to God that he may clean you, prune you and refine you. God does this because glory is destructive to the immature. Maturity is built in His presence, and it makes you ready to carry God's glory.

Printed in Great Britain
by Amazon

64700021R00108